I0490501

Passive Income Ideas

*The Ultimate Guide to Make Money
Online, Expand Your Business and Achieve
The Freedom you Desire, Discover the Best
Ideas and Strategies to Start Generate
Passive Income in 2020*

Author Name: Harvey Quick

Description

When was the last time you had a vacation? A work-free enjoyable holiday, maybe to the Bahamas with your family for a whole week or more? Wait, can you even afford such? If your answer to both is *never,* then the *Passive Income Ideas* handbook is about to change your way of hustle.

Many people look forward to attaining financial freedom in their lives but are not sure of how to achieve that, or where to start. The internet has frustrated you with promises of making millions over a couple of days. Maybe you've tried some of those ways in vain, and you're sitting there wondering if you were born to retire underemployment.

Worry no more. This handbook is here to give you insights on the best ways to turn your bank statements around. The book introduces you to passive income and how it's your only way out of that day job. You'll get to learn how passive income works and ways to come up with lucrative business ideas.

If you don't have the capital, this handbook will give you several ways to acquire capital for your business or investment. If you don't have any business ideas in mind, this book has 21 lucrative ideas. Even if you have so much capital but are scared of misspending, this book shows you precautions to take with your money. It tells you who to trust in business, and who to watch out for. When to partner up and when to go solo.

Getting into business is not an easy thing to do; not when you are clueless about the industries. But with this handbook, you get an introduction to various business industries, how they work, and how they generate money. It's not the backend for making three figures overnight, but it's the ultimate blueprint to starting your journey of earning passive income from the comfort of your couch.

The good thing is, all the business ideas given in this book entail working less and earning more just as passive income ventures should be. By investing in them you will have time for family, friends and for self-growth. Say goodbye to long working hours, being overworked and underpaid and living life as a routine.

Industries are waiting for you to launch that big idea. All you need to do is click that download button. Not convinced yet? Here is a sneak peek of what the book entails.

Inside you'll find;

- What passive income is and how you've been going wrong all your life working day and night for a minimal lifestyle
- The S.M.A.R.T formula and how to use it to achieve your goals
- How to find the best passive income venture that will keep you motivated
- 21 different types of business ideas explained from what they entail, if they are worth your time, what you need to get started and how to earn from them
- How to overcome your fear of investment. You can do this!
- Stop worrying about investment options. Get tips on how to start small and how to start big for those with money
- Don't have a dime to invest? Here are solid suggestions on where to find capital

Table of Contents

Introduction

Congratulations on purchasing *Passive Income Ideas* and thank you for doing so.

The following chapters will discuss ways in which you can switch your hustle from active to passive income. For decades now, most of us have spent our lives working from dusk till dawn trying to make ends meet with just bills and basic needs. You've probably never experienced the relief of a vacation or even an eight-hour sleep.

Financial freedom? A totally foreign phrase to you. This is a result of the active income lifestyle. That's why I wrote this handbook. To help you get out of your comfort zone and think outside the box. I mean who doesn't want to work less but earn more every day? Employment won't give you that.

Hence, Passive Income Ideas is your go-to handbook that breaks down all the aspects of approaching specific ventures that give you the freedom to work anywhere in the world, earn over five times more than your current income, vacation any day without the need to plan for it twelve months earlier, and finally give you more time for a social life and a good night's sleep.

Say goodbye to your sleepless nights, crazy bills and debts that suck out your energy. The tips in this book are very transparent and the guide as accurate as possible.

There are plenty of books on this subject on the market, thanks again for choosing this one! Every effort was made to ensure it is full of as much useful information as possible, please enjoy!

Chapter 1: What is Passive Income?

To understand what passive income is, you need to go back to the basics. There are three types of income - Active, Passive and Portfolio Income. For centuries, passive income has been associated with income acquired from ventures where an individual is not directly or actively involved. Active income is the immediate opposite of passive income in that it's earned when an individual directly performs a service. Portfolio income is income earned when an individual invests. In portfolio income, we look at money earned in interests, as dividends, royalties and the like. In most cases, as well as in this book, passive and portfolio income is addressed as one; since they both embrace some similar aspects.

Analyzing Passive Income

The definition of passive income does not rule it out as work; it only means that you get to work less as compared to when employed at a business. That your hours are not 9 to 5; they may be more, they may be less. The idea is you cannot compare it with an active worker who earns less and works more. The effort an active worker puts in your job, almost never matches their income. As for a passive worker, they work less and earn more. However, if they work more, then they double their earnings. You can simply conclude that a passive worker gets income every time they put effort into their venture, and sometimes even in their sleep.

To get into passive income, you need an investment or a venture. The idea can range from yours to someone else's. If the idea is yours, you can higher contractors to work on the technicalities and earn from that. If the idea is someone else's, then you can simply earn from the person's efforts. The venture can also be an already existing business owned by someone else, or a business on sale.

The Internal Revenue Service (IRS) takes on Passive Income

The IRS takes the passive income understanding into a deeper level by defining passive activity as any business participation where the taxpayer is not materially involved. Material involvement, according to the IRS, is continuous, regular, and substantial. Material involvement encompasses the following:

- More than 500 hours of activity toward the venture
- Participating in all activities of the tax year
- Participating as much as everyone else in the business, and about 100+ hours
- Constant material involvement in the last five to ten years of the business' tax years

- For those in personal serviced businesses, you should have at least 3 years of material involvement in any previous tax years

The IRS has categorized passive income into two; rentals and businesses. When it comes to rentals, they have included both real estate and equipment used. As long as the taxpayer does not materially participate in any of these two categories, then their venture is defined as that of passive income.

Below are a few examples of passive income ventures:

1. Real Estate
2. Leasing of Equipment
3. Limited Partnerships
4. Silent investment in partnerships and LLCs
5. Peer to peer lending
6. Online businesses
7. Dividend stocks

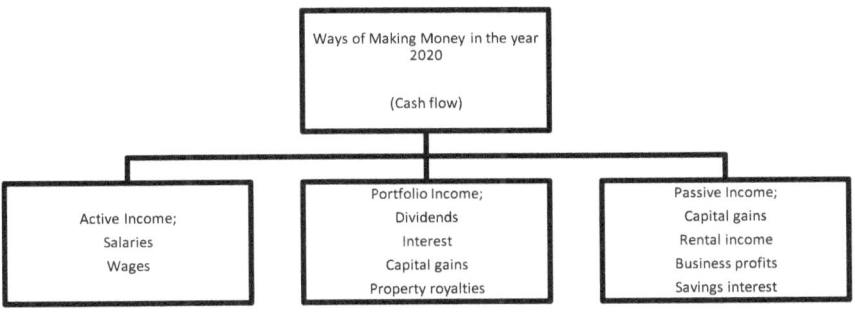

Passive Income is, therefore, the amount earned by passive taxpayers and can be categorized into 2; dividends and capital gains.

What is a Dividend?

This is an amount out of a company's profits, that's regularly paid to the shareholders.

What is Capital Gain?

Capital gains are profits made from selling an investment or property. To determine investment or property, look at a company's capital assets. Capital assets include vehicles, rental properties, machinery, furniture, trademarks, stock, debentures, and goodwill among many others.

Take an example:
Company X has 3 motor vehicles that they no longer need, so they decide to sell them off. The amount of profit they make from selling the three cars is therefore referred to as a capital gain. Any capital asset sold that brings about profit results in a capital gain.

While that example cleanly explains a capital gain, there's always a higher probability that some assets, like the motor vehicles, can't bring about capital gains. This is due to their nature of depreciation. Motor vehicles lose value probably the minute you buy them as they immediately are considered "second hand". Therefore, when you sell them, they bring about a loss from the initial buying price. With that said, note that it is possible to experience capital loss as well.

How the IRS Taxes Capital Gains

The IRS has divided capital gains into short term and long term tax categories, based on their ownership of a capital asset. If a business holds an investment for at most a year, it's considered a short term investment. On the other hand, if a business holds an investment for more than one year, they are considered long term assets.

The new tax plan brought about lower taxes for businesses and individuals. It also contains lower corporate tax rates and a handful of tax deductions. Now, short term investments are taxed just at the usual income tax rates while long term investments are taxed lower than the regular income tax rate.

The IRS has categorized taxpayers into 4:
- Single
- Married and filing jointly
- Married but filing separately
- Head of household

Current tax rates for this category are; 10%, 12%, 22%, 24%, 32%, 35%, and 37%. Single taxpayers fall under the 10% tax bracket while 37% is the highest tax bracket that only applies to capital gains that go above $510,301 per year for a single taxpayer.

As mentioned, long term investments are those held for over a year and taxed at either 0%, 15%, or 20% depending on an individual's income bracket. A single taxpayer is taxed 0% if they earn below $39,375. If a single filler earns above $39,375 but below $434,550 as annual income and decides to sell their assets, the IRS will charge the individual a 15% tax rate on those profits. You can tell that long term assets are more affordable tax-wise as compared to short term assets and investments.

When you venture into a passive income business, you'll enjoy the freedom of time and place. As mentioned earlier, most passive businesses can be managed remotely and do not require 12 hours a day of working. This means you'll be able to vacation all you want and have personal time.

You probably want this because you're looking into the future and wondering how retirement will hold up for you. Not just retirement but also life for your children. To secure your future on a financial level, it's important to invest in something that does not require a direct effort to bring income.

Relieve yourself off employment stress. It's quite obvious how many suffer under the hands of the 9 to 5 working system. It probably drains out all your energy and brings about a boring vibe with its monotonous daily routine. At least with passive income, you can quit your job and work when you want or need to.

Earn more. It's evident that most passive income businesses bring more income as compared to salaries. If an investment can earn you an extra $5000 per month and you earn a salary of $4000 a month, you'll be able to save up and leave work sooner than eventually planned.

Just because passive income businesses seem so enticing, doesn't mean they are easy to take part in. Depending on which one you're interested in, it may be beneficial to learn the industry and how it works, for the sake of making better decisions with your money and investment choices.

Chapter 2: Understanding and Developing a Positive Mindset

A positive mindset is more about one's overall perspective on something and a tendency to focus on all that is good in it. It is a mental and emotional attitude that focuses on the bright side of situations and expects positive results.

As an investor, one ought' to be positive even when facing the most critical challenges. It is in such situations that you can get a breakthrough. The challenges should make us more creative than break us. It can even unlock the best strategy one could ever have.

A growth mindset sees opportunities beyond limits. It defies all the parameters of any particular state of things. The mindset makes investors and entrepreneurs think in a more creative and innovative way hence enabling them to progress. It brings out the best of determination and vigor one has to deal with a negative situation. As a business leader, the growth mindset acts as a motivating factor to keep you doing what you are doing.

Negative thinking or pessimism, in other words, is a mental attitude of anticipating the worst of any possible outcomes on situations. It is the ability of the mind to produce unfavorable thoughts to what a person needs.

Disadvantages of a Negative Mindset in a Business Setting

It discourages hard work

Always expecting the worst from a given situation sometimes means being discouraged from being successful. Don't be the type of businessperson who says, "After all, if it isn't going to happen, why the need to strive towards it?"

Stifled creativity

When in constant negativity, you probably won't push towards thinking differently. Without thinking about improving upon a given situation, you fail on innovativeness.

A fixed mindset operates within the present state of things. Being fixed minded always means that as an investor, you are destined to fail and eventually give up. It makes you narrow down your thinking instead of seeing the possibility of growth.

Tips on Achieving a Positive Mindset

Be open-minded

Opening your mind to the possibilities of new opportunities and knowledge enhances success to investors. Being open-minded mostly involves two factors, finding your ultimate motivation and choosing the areas to develop.

In order for you to facilitate the embracing of new ideas, you first of all need to motivate yourself into trying new things. This involves knowing why you want to be more open if you have that commitment to it and also the willingness to execute it to make it happen.

In choosing the areas to develop, you have to narrow down to one scope of investing to explore new ideas and slowly include more in a bigger perspective of the venture. Starting small majorly results in having an open mind, instead of making a sudden, change into your investment. A positive attitude towards new experiences lets you open up to discoveries regularly.

Be more proactive and less reactive
Reactive business strategies respond to some unanticipated event only after it occurs, while proactive strategies anticipate possible challenges. A business that dwells mostly on a proactive strategy is deemed to deal with challenges more effectively. They allow a business the liberty to decide on matters regarding them rather than responding in the aftermath of a situation i.e. reactive strategy.
Let's take for example how a property owner insures his property against fire.

The insurance is more of a proactive technique to take care of peril in case it may arise. If a fire arises and destroys the property, a reactive individual could probably call for firefighters and this means suffering from more losses as it takes time. For the proactive case, an insurance claim makes the owner back on track unlike the other who goes down. The insurance ensures continuity of business. This is indeed positivity.

Basically, the distinguishing factor between applying a proactive strategy and a reactive strategy basically involves being prepared and accountable. Too much focus on proactive strategies, however, could be wasteful if the anticipated trends are not accurately forecast, or if the anticipated and planned-for events never occur. Reactive strategies avoid this problem by focusing on a situation that is currently active, thus reducing unnecessary effort or wasteful allocation of resources.

Thinking big

Means you are more likely to achieve a goal that goes beyond your expectations. It draws people who have the same attitude. The bigger the thinking the more success you achieve. Think about how you can develop the imaginary thoughts into reality by letting the ideas flow freely and take note of the greatest idea then invest in that.

If you are capable of thinking outside of the box, it would mean that you are defying all odds. Much success is achieved as mediocrity is dealt with. A business thinking in that angle is able to thrive in all situations over its competitors as it takes account of extra perspective the others don't.

Thinking big also brings about a team that shares ideas as well as make positive plans are and ultimately grows leaders out of the team and even promoting them to new heights in their career. Thinking big begins with boundary-pushing hence dream-inspiring attitude at the end of it.

Be more persuasive and less manipulative

Manipulation treats persuasion as an intention to fool or control another party of the conversation into doing or believing in your school of thought hence leaving them influenced. It works just as a bribe meaning you might be concealing an idea.

For example, if you are a real estate marketer then you come across prospective tenants. Let's say a family of seven and they need a unit of a house only - you then go ahead to propose a mansion with a lawn, probably a bit expensive that would mean more commission. But, instead of building a conversation on the benefits of the lawn, you talk of the house alone. This would be manipulation. You are supposed to say even that the lawn could benefit the children. Make the customer see it. It should seem like you are hiding something.

Persuasiveness underlies intent hence creating the difference between persuasive and manipulative strategy.

Be bold and confident

Doing something boldly and with confidence makes you a mark rather than leaving you stuck in the same old pattern and immune to positive change. It is all about getting things done with a positive attitude. You need to be able to move and work with that sense. Confidence has the ability to inspire reaching for new horizons in all we aspire to do both in life and business.

A simple example of this is driving a car. Most people who have been driving for some time do so almost automatically and confidently. This contrasts with a first-time driver who will probably feel nervous. He or she lacks confidence in their ability to drive. Gaining confidence and taking the first step can be very difficult. Often the thought of starting something new is worse than doing it. This is where apart from the confidence the preparation, learning and thinking positively can also help, as previously stated.

A bold attitude means everything in business. It is the powerhouse for ensuring a positive response to the challenges we face regularly. It builds us and our teams and even broods the enjoyment in it.

Benefits of Having a Positive Mindset

There are a lot of interviews involving successful business people and leaders all over social platforms. They hold great content most of the time. Probably we go through them hoping that sooner or later we will be like them. However, one thing is for sure; we should not pick on what they do, but look keenly into how they do what they do. It is almost impossible to assume that all successful entrepreneurs are positive people; probably any of them got there with anything less than a positive attitude.

The question is; could success be as a result of positive thinking?

Helps in problem-solving

Research has found out that those who dwell much on thinking positively have a better chance to take in new information which in turn improves one's point of view and ability to relate to matters hence, enabling them to deal with any problems or challenges that may come up. Regardless of how huge a problem could be, a positive thinker tries hard not to see things from that angle. He or she will try hard to find a solution and not run from it taking into consideration that is what makes him or her, what he or she is. Actually puts himself or herself into the shoe to solve it in the most accurate way.

Positive thinkers have more energy

Positive thinking means a positive dispositional affect hence more energy and enthusiasm against those who have more negative affectivity. The dispositional effect is the trait of seeing things from a positive or negative point of view. Positivity makes one give the best of what he or she is made of. A positive investor still finds the strength to go the extra mile in investing even in the harshest of times. Failing to keep with the race would probably mean the end of a venture.

Positivity builds resilience

Many entrepreneurs hardly succeed in their first business idea or venture. They take even years. They face many hurdles, fail and make many mistakes before actually making it to the top of business. Studies have shown that positivity can push you towards becoming more resilient. Despite falling numerous times, a positive entrepreneur keeps on trying over and over again hoping to ultimately succeed at the end of it all. Success actually is meant to take time as it is said, good things take time. One has to keep on grinding harder

Positive thinking improves decision making

It is more than obvious that if you are a negative-minded kind of person, you cannot make decisions that bring about a positive impact. To be precise, negative thinking in the entrepreneurial world could probably lead to decisions likely to harm a venture. Being positive unlocks a perspective where one is able to see deeper into situations. This enables the formulation of ideal decisions.

Positivity is infectious... Even in the workplace

Positivity among entrepreneurs with direct engagement with their customers gives them a higher convincing power to persuade them (customers) to try a new product. It is contagious. This is almost true if not a fact. Take for instance a manager using negative words and even acting in the same manner, he or she is more likely to infect the juniors too. A leader is meant to make the subjects greater than he or she is which means he or she has to pass on whatever good is in possession to impact them.

Positive thinking however on its own means nothing if it's not going to be put into action.

Chapter 3: Turning Your Passion into a Business

Are you on a 9 to 5 job, that's draining the life out of you? Or maybe you are almost out of college and would like to venture into a field that makes you smile even in the hardest days? Then turning your passion into a business is the way to go, however, turning your passion into a business is not easy and the journey ahead requires patience and most importantly commitment.

If you enjoy singing, or maybe you are into sports, or maybe you are into programming but find yourself working in a financial institution. The time to turn that passion into a business is now. Read on as we go through some of the things you need to consider before turning your passion into a business as well as steps to turn that passion into a money-making endeavor.

But before that, let's find out why turning that passion into a money-making venture is way better.

- Gives you more fulfillment and joy, research has shown that about 35% of people who engage in hobbies are less depressed. Having time to do things one loves has also been shown to increase one's overall well-being.
- You get to manage your time and spend time on things and people who matter to you, the busy schedules may sometimes be overwhelming as a result neglecting family

time, self-improvement or development of other skills. Turning that passion into a business allows you to plan your time. You do not have to worry about rushing every day before family breakfast or missing your child's dance performance.

- Ability to develop other skills, turning your passion into a business gives you time to excel and grow your skills, for instance, if you are passionate about garment making, starting a business in this field requires you to work on garments each day ensuring you become the best at your passion.

- You get to make a difference in society, for your passion to become a successful business venture it is important to provide something new and bring solutions. This gives you an opportunity to make a difference in your area as well as bring out the best version of you, making life more fulfilling and happier.

- Working on your passion makes you more innovative in turn brings greater success, though there are low and hard moments in any business working on something you enjoy lessens the dull days and may influence a different and better approach to solving the problems.

Feeling motivated enough to take that big step and turn your passion into an enterprise, below are 6 things to consider before turning your passion into a business.

1. Find out whether your passion can generate income, the aim of turning your passion into a business is to generate sustainable and long term income. For instance, if your passion is baking, then start by sharing your products with your colleagues, family, and friends. This will help you establish what will work in the market and how best to introduce your products or services to the market.

2. Will you provide a solution? This is an important question before venturing into business, and more so before turning what you love to do to an enterprise, providing a solution and new experience gives you a competitive advantage and allows easy entry into the market.

3. Flexibility, for you to turn your passion into a successful business venture it is essential to have an open mind, you can only experience real growth in your business once you apply needed changes. Some of the most successful businesses across the globe are open to change.

4. Consider your financial situation, starting a business might take a toll on your finances, especially if you are on your own, thus important to ensure you are in a stable financial place for the smooth running of the business.

5. What is your aim? Finding out the reason behind turning your passion into a business will greatly help in ensuring you join an entrepreneur for all the right things. Running a business is not easy, and joining a business with the wrong mindset and attitude might set you up for failure. Find out whether you are ready and most importantly have the patience to see your business grow.

6. Are you good at your skills? If you are going to turn your passion into a business, then you need to be the best at it, so take time to practice and be an expert. As you practice, find a mentor to guide you through.

Consider various financial investors, starting up a business without financial assistance may be draining, to avoid this, create a marketing strategy and pitch your idea to potential investors, this will not only lessen your financial load but will also provide a new voice to the business.

Once you have identified why you want to start this business and how to make it a success it is now time to turn it into reality.

Steps to Turning your Passion into a Business

Make the move; after you have done your research about the market prices, and desired location, it's time to make the first move. The first step is filled with emotions, happiness, doubt, wondering whether you will make it. Will people buy your products? There is no other way to find out other than making that first move.

Have a team, have people on your side who will help turn your idea into a million-dollar industry, though it might take time, having a strong foundation will help boost your business. For the best result allow dialogue before the onset of the business, though the idea is yours always remember your team members might share a fresh and new perspective. If this is not possible, engage your friends and family and find out what they think about the venture. Also consider joining social groups in the same field, attend forums and workshops, but always remember to stay focused on the end goal.

Market your business, let people know about your business, marketing has been made easier with the use of technology, you can now showcase your products using social media platforms, with platforms such as Facebook, Instagram, Twitter or LinkedIn you connect with people all over the world.

Set your work schedules, since you no longer have someone telling you what time you need to report or leave the office it is important to set working hours and abide by them. Staying motivated as an entrepreneur requires discipline and motivation and to ensure your business grows it is vital to put in the time.

Learn more about business and more so your venture, maybe it's your first time in the entrepreneurial world. There is more to business than passion, find out more about your clientele, research on marketing strategies that will work for your business and find out more about legal matters concerning your business.

Get in touch with your suppliers, before embarking on this journey it is vital to settle on a supplier, however before settling be sure to find out the best prices in the market, you can find a wholesale supplier on eBay, Google or through business groups.

Financial planning, consider investing in a qualified accountant to help with the calculations, have proper documentation on capital invested, profit margins and fixed prices this will help in preventing major losses and setting of prices for your products or services.

Find several streams of income, to avoid a strain on your business, venture into other passive income streams that will allow you time for your business to grow. There are several business ideas that require little involvement and may be a good stepping stone towards a successful business. You may consider blogging, being a virtual part-time assistant, tutoring, just to mention a few.

Be patient, starting a business requires patience and in some cases might need three to six months before picking up, do not give up.

Stay informed, to stay on top of the game, having relevant information on the business is key. Subscribe to newsletter that gives weekly or daily business updates, this will increase your knowledge of business, in turn, promoting growth.

Avoid distractions and negativity, running a business is not easy and along the way, you will encounter negative voice, have a support system, stay positive and always remember your end goal.

Though your passion promotes your well-being turning it to a business may be hard and time consuming, in turn causing stress and burn out, to avoid this, create a work-life balance, set a plan, a good way to achieve your plans and still enjoy time with family and friends is writing down a to-do list, a good approach would be writing your monthly to-do list, then break down the list to weekly goals and for the best results break down the list further to daily goal. Also, remember to be realistic in the goals.

Chapter 4: Turning Your Favorite Activity into a Business

A hobby is an activity done in your free time for leisure purposes. There are many life skills that you may have as hobbies but can also be used as a source of income. Some of them include baking web design, photography, and painting among others. The truth is, you may be afraid to start due to fear of failure but this should not hinder you from achieving your goal.

Create a Plan

You need to come up with a concrete plan for you to bring your business into reality. Determine whether you just need a side hustle or you will venture full time. Write a business plan and evaluate how much you need to start and run your business, and also use it to assess outcomes. Create a strategy and start working on your hobby part-time, by working evenings and weekends, while saving the cash to go full time in the future. Using the business plan, outline where your business is now and the goals you are willing to achieve. Consider diversifying the services in order to get more income. This means that if your hobby is baking, you can sell cakes and also offer baking classes. Whichever plan you use, ensure that it is smart and that it works.

Plan your first sale

Whether you make 1 dollar or 5,000 dollars, your first sale is the most important sale for your business. Your first clients boost your confidence and give you the morale to carry on. Depending on the product or service you are selling, you need to come up with the best strategy for making your brand known. You may decide to offer a free trial so as to study the market and get feedback. Ensure you market your products on low budget platforms e.g. social media to increase visibility.

Create time for your business

To be practical it's not easy working a full-time job and then pursuing a hobby as a side hustle. Between family, social life and personal commitment, you do not have enough time in a day to take care of business. Before deciding whether you want to pursue your hobby full time, you need to be creative about how you use your time.

You may need to wake up a little early and sleep late for your business to succeed. Where possible you may involve your family to assist so as to get more work done. Hobbies are done during free time but once they become a business, you need to be more intentional so as to succeed.

Build an online presence

All business today requires an online presence not only for visibility but also for feedback and convenience. A functional website together with a social media profile will go a long way in taking your business to the next level. The website should have a clear message on what you are selling, be easy to navigate and have a contact page for clients to reach you.

Being consistent in the way you present your brand is important and a content creation plan should be developed. Only quality images of your products should be displayed online and you can hire professionals to do it for you. Digital marketing should be done intensively on all platforms. Facebook is a good platform to start marketing your products as it is free and your friends will become your first clients.

Build a network

As the saying goes, 'Your network is your net worth'. For your business to grow, you need to engage in self-promotion since word of mouth travels very first. It is important to find clubs and groups in your area of specialization so that you can engage with other professionals in your niche.

Be prepared on matters pertaining to your business as other people will like to hear how you started and where you are currently. Have a short elevator speech in mind to market your brand and also offer help in a networking session as everyone needs to help one way or another. Always take contacts where possible to follow up and consult later.

Treat your hobby like a job

In order for your hobby to succeed as a business, you have to give it all the attention and seriousness it deserves. This will ensure it brings you a substantial second income or even become your main source of income someday. Set time apart from your schedule to work on your hobby and research widely on the industry it falls in.

Start today as procrastinating for too long may make you talk yourself out of starting the business. When you turn your hobby into a job, ensure that you still enjoy doing it as it will now involve meeting deadlines and dealing with difficult clients. It will also come with a lot of responsibilities e.g. marketing and managing finances.

Remember the more you want from your business, the harder you have to work. Ensure you perfect what you do and even make plans to improve your skills through further training.

Create a brand and stick to it

Branding is just as important for small businesses as it is for big companies. There exists a link between strong branding and successful businesses. You should come up with a functional business name logo and color scheme, and they should all be a reflection of your business.

Use these components consistently on your website, social media pages and in all your branding materials. This increases visibility and helps your loyal customers to recognize you. When customers connect emotionally with your brand, they tend to be more loyal and advocate for your brand. This in return leads to better sales and business growth.

Market your business extensively

The secret to home business success aside from offering great services is marketing. People will only buy from you if they are aware of your products and services. You should create a marketing plan and make marketing activities a part of your everyday schedule.

Identify your target customers and look at ways that you can attract them to your business. Consider conducting market research to determine whether there is a ready market for your goods and services. As much as turning your hobby into a business is fun, it should be treated professionally so as to make a living out of it.

Make your Business legal

The process of registering your business is quite straightforward. It is important to comply with local and state regulations to avoid legal hassles. While naming your business, it is necessary to check with the registrar of companies to ensure that your name isn't already taken.

You may register your business as a sole proprietorship or as a limited liability company (LLC).It can also be a partnership if you intend to go into business with someone else. Ensure you have all the necessary permits required to ensure your business runs smoothly. Regardless of your business structure, ensure you have a separate business bank account for all your finances.

Factors to Consider Before Turning Your Hobby into a Business

Is it the right time for a transition?

Although we say that the right time to begin is now, turning a hobby into a business requires planning and perfect timing. You need to evaluate how many hours you need out of your normal schedule to run the business. If you have a lot of things going on in your life e.g. a newborn or paying off a debt, then it may not be the best time to transition.

Are you ready to turn your dream into a reality?

We all have dreams but when it comes to doing the actual work, a lot of persistence is required. You should develop a list of all that is required of you in the business and then make a decision from there.

Can you actually make money?

While money isn't always a priority for everyone, you will most likely continue pursuing a venture if it is bringing in money. You need to determine whether your hobby will turn into a paycheck for you to pay your bills. Consider visiting a financial consultant to give advice on the options available, risks involved and opportunities for growth.

Can you take criticism positively?

You need to establish whether you are ready to accept feedback from your clients, family, and friends whether positive or negative. It's good to accept that people will always have an opinion on your business and how you should run it.

Can you work part-time alongside your full-time job?

If you are not ready to leave your part-time job, you will need to work part-time and this could be very exhausting. This, however, provides time to lay a foundation for the growth of your business before you venture into it full time.

Turning a hobby into a business could take away the fun from something you once loved. It's important to conduct research and weigh all available options before you quit your job to pursue this venture. With the right planning, dedication and the right attitude, transitioning can be very easy. A lot of effort should be placed on learning the dynamics of starting and running a business to ensure success.

Chapter 5: Using the formula S.M.A.R.T

Setting up a business requires a constructive plan to ensure everything is planned for and a clear direction dictates everything the business does. You have to cater to every emergency that may come up and be prepared to deal with changes in the business plan and adjustment of your own goals to suit your projected business direction. Setting a business plan should be concrete and not sound like well-intentioned wishes. To enable you to clarify your business goals, use the SMART formulae, which is a time tested method of aligning one's goals with the available resources. SMART is an acronym for Specific, Measurable, Appropriate, Realistic and Timely. Some people add an extra letter, 'P' for passion but this is not standard.

Specific

Goals such as making a profit, hiring better employees or expanding are non-specific goals and merely communicate an intention rather than a specific goal to attain something. However, when these goals take on more definitions such as reducing overhead costs by 10%, or increasing market size to at least 15%, they increase their specificity and this makes them more focused on the overall goal.

It is difficult to attain all goals one set their eyes on, but it is possible to focus on just a few goals and make sure you attain them. This is why it is important to constantly check on the progress of your goals and whether they are still within limit. You are allowed to adjust your expectations to conform to external realities, however, conforming does not mean abandoning your goals, it just means changing your tactics towards attaining them.

Having specific goals does not mean you stifle any chances of innovation or pivoting to better products. In some instances, you might stumble upon a new product that has yet to attain prime popularity. However, your gut instincts may tell you to get into that business and to trust it. Sometimes aversion to risk can be a good thing just as much as it can be bad. People who avoid risk also miss out on a lot of opportunities in business. It is difficult to be specific or to create objectively specific goals when the product is risky and you are fueled by your gut instincts alone. However, the goal is to put some sort of metrics on your objectives in order to trace your path to success better.

Measurable

All goals should be measurable. This not only increases their specificity but also increases their attainability. Ensure you state your goals so that any third party observer can measure them objectively. For example, 'we will hire 15 more people in the next quarter.' This is an example of a measurable goal whose attainability is independent of the subject. It is attained once the measure is met. In order to achieve something great, it is important for you to have multiple measurable goals. You, therefore, need tools to measure your goals. In most cases, the units of measure are in numbers.

For example, thirty days, 40 orders, 50 new customers, etc. These are units that are objectively easy to measure. However, some measures can be slightly complicated. For example, measuring customer satisfaction requires quantifiable units as well as proper knowledge of human behavior. The number of positive direct feedback measures customer satisfaction and also by checking the number of return customers, churn rate and referrals you get. You can get many referrals, make zero sales, and end up blaming your products when perhaps it is your pricing or website user interface that is the problem.

Appropriate

Appropriate goals are goals that are within your own area of responsibility. You cannot seek to attain a goal that is under the job description of someone else. For example, as a human resource professional you cannot have a goal such as 'To reduce overheads by 10%'. The goals also have to be aligned with one another in the same organization. The human resource manager cannot have a goal of increasing the number of employees by 25%, whilst the finance department has a goal of reducing labor costs by 35%. These two goals cancel each other out.

Your goals should also align with your skills and capacity to deliver. Though this is a difficult concept for most people to accept because it is a measure (critique) of their abilities, it is essential that you are aware of your own limitations. This does not mean that seeking to achieve more is bad, it only means that before making a decision to go beyond your own capability, you should first measure your resources, skills, and passion before making such a decision. In most cases, other people are dependent on you as a business owner, not to make mistakes.

Realistic

Set realistic goals so that meeting them does not become an impossible task. Even though it is advisable to aim higher, your aim should not be too unrealistic from a skill point of view or even a financial resources standpoint. Starting a business merely on the basis of hope or faith rarely works. It is important to be certain of your resources before you can even attempt to achieve something beyond the expected measure of attainment. Research helps in attuning your expectations and aligning your resources with your expected outcomes. In some businesses, it is possible to achieve way above what is expected; whereas in others it is important that you keep your goals within reasonable limits otherwise you may overexpose your resources to risk and kill the business.

Always remember to refer to your company's resources and your own skills in using these resources to meet your objective. You alone know best how and when to utilize your skills, and by simply keeping true to yourself, you can increase your skill level and at the same time increase your business productivity. For example, it is unrealistic to create marketing videos without a background in marketing or even advertising. However spending some time researching and learning, will increase your skill level to a point you become an expert in the matter. Your skill levels will then be capable of creating highly impactful marketing material for your business. View all unrealistic goals as challenges to improve yourself.

Timely

Always ensure you put a deadline on all your goals even if some of them might sound lofty. A goal such as 'retire by the age of 35' sounds more concrete and realistic than, 'retire when I am rich.' Always ensure you keep on checking your deadlines and remember it is okay to adjust deadlines if they are difficult to meet. As a business owner, you know best where to adjust and how to adjust based on your research and experience. Other market forces will also determine how you adjust or even completely change your goals and plans. So long as your end goal remains attainable, you can adjust timetables to fit your immediate reality.

In setting a framework for deadlines, remember to work backward calculating risk and resources before meeting goals to the starting point. Set a deadline that depends on something else being met. For example, you can say, 'By January next year I need to increase product portfolio to 5 products.' This in itself is a good goal and attainable.

However, if you say, "By next year I need to increase product portfolio to 5 product once I break even,' you will have a better matrix of judging the success of your business. Here you have set two goals in one without increasing expectations or risks.

If the overall goal seems too difficult or overwhelming, it is okay to break them up into smaller attainable goals. These smaller goals can then be divided amongst a group of people within your company or you can work on all of them so long as you have a proper working timetable to capture each one.

The SMART formula may not have a basis in sound economic theory but it has helped many businesses to outline their goals in a manner that assures them greater chances of success. However, without passion, these goals and processes outlined in the SMART formula will not work.

Passion is the fuel that drives your business whereas the SMART formula is merely the road. If your business is the car, you need fuel first before you can embark on the road to your journey.

Passion ensures your business does not stop even when other external factors stop. Even in the absence of resources, passion ensures you work hard to attain them and to keep your business afloat until the next resources are available.

More businesses have failed due to a lack of passion than lack of plans or resources. Therefore it is important to realize that you should at least want your business to succeed before you set up any concrete plans that will require your time, money and attention. The SMART formula focuses your business and makes it easier to determine which aspects of it are working and which ones are not.

Chapter 6: Venturing Into Passive Activity on Low Budget

Passive income ventures are known to bring quite a lump sum with just minimal to no material involvement of an investor. However, you'd need to squint to find such ventures that do not require capital or some sort of investment amount. While some partners may choose to invest with their knowledge and skills only, in most businesses, partners request some type of monetary input.

This means that for you to tap into the passive income sector, you'll need some sort of cash. Luckily, not all passive business activities require millions of dollars of investment. But since there are hundreds of passive ventures, it's important that your first step to being identifying the passive income ideas that require a small budget to start or invest. With the perfect idea in mind, the rest becomes a walk in the park.

Picking a Small Budget Venture

In chapters three and four of this handbook, you were able to learn the different ways in which you can create passive income with your favorite activity or something you're truly passionate about. Keep those two factors in mind as we try to narrow down to ideas that are cheap to venture in. Don't get it twisted, just because an idea is passive and affordable, it does not mean that it is easy to handle or its success easy to attain.

Whether you're dealing with a low budget idea or a big budget venture, you'll require determination and smart analysis to prosper. It just means that their small nature makes them either require more time to bring in some great returns, or you may start earning fast but in tiny bits as it grows.

Here are a few small-budget ideas listed:
- Start a blog
- Write and publish an eBook
- Create an online course
- Become an affiliate marketer
- Build a sales funnel
- Develop an application
- Generate royalties from audio tracks
- Create YouTube video tutorials
- Sell photos online
- Peer to peer lending platforms

From the above list, you can make an easy conclusion that the most affordable passive income ideas are online ideas. In 2020, it is believed that most types of investments will be done online. Here's the thing about working online; it's not just easy since you can work from home or travel work, resources required are minimal and affordable. Most of what you'll invest in is time and energy.

Take starting a blog for example.

With a good and lucrative blog idea, all you need is the following:

- Internet connection
- Domain and hosting
- Get a blog developed or develop it using easy platforms like WordPress and Six that do not require programming knowledge
- Have a good camera or phone that can take HD images for your blog
- Invest in blog post editors like Grammarly that ensure your work is neat and not plagiarized.

Aside from that, the writing process, photography, posting and social media is all the effort and time you put out. The 5 requirements will never add to millions of money, making it possible for anyone to start a blog. When you consider cash flow aspects of a blog, it may take up to 6 months for a blogger to earn their first coin.

A newbie without blogging knowledge can take up to a year or more to earn from it. So you can add a blogging course to the investment list. With blogging knowledge, a beautifully designed blog, interesting posts, a personality that people love to associate with, and constant social media activity, you may start earning less than six months in.

When it comes to earning, as earlier mentioned, you won't hit the big numbers with your first earning. However, it depends on the venture. A blogger who hits the charts so fast might be approached by corporations for product promotions or ambassadorship. This means you'll earn good money on your first count. However, others might make as low as $50 after six to twelve months.

Ways to Gather Small Budget Capital

Once you've selected a viable and suitable small budget passive income idea, do some intensive research on the idea. This research is to find out two things; one, what it entails and if you're willing to go through its hurdles and two, how much you need to invest in it. Never start a business, no matter which one, without a budget analysis of the requirements. Also, ensure the budget analysis includes some miscellaneous amount.

You don't need to hire a professional to draft a budget for you. This is something you can achieve on your own. The first step is to write a list of things you may need to start the business. The second step is to research different vendors of the services and compare their rates. Thirdly, draft a budget and arrive at the total you'll need.

How to Choose the Best Vendors

Before selecting the companies that will serve your business, it's important to take a few tips into consideration:

Go through their entire website to see what they are all about. It's rarely advisable to choose a company that offers your required service as a minority among their services. This would mean one of two things; either they are not so good at it, or lack enough resources to offer it as should or it's a new feature of their services so it's a work in progress. A company that only offers the specific services or majors in it, would be in a better position to offer you the best from expertise to resources.

Avoid new companies. While this is negativity towards new companies that keeps them from growing, you have to look out for yourself and mot try and roll the dice with your investment. This leads you to the third most important point

Check their portfolio. A reputable company will have their portfolio on their website for all prospects to see. In case they don't have, you can email them for a few of their previous jobs. Look into the companies they have worked for or with to ensure that their expertise matches what you're looking for. This means that if a company is new but has one or two great portfolios, you may consider working with them but under lenient terms. If a company does not have a portfolio, click out of their site and move to the next. Your money is as valuable as your time.

Ask about any hidden charges. Some companies like to attract the prospect's eye them doom their pockets when the deal is done. If their quotation seems suspicious, ask questions or move along. You want to work with a company that is 100% transparent.

Don't be tempted by the low costs. It is assumed that some companies charge way too low because their expertise does not match up those of executive corporates. After approving their skills by checking their portfolio, ask for a breakdown of their charges. Anyone can tell an underrated or overrated quotation. Don't be scared to add a few dollars to your investment budget just to get legitimate vendors. It's always worth it.

What is their response time? If a company takes more than 5 hours to respond to your inquiry, question their efficiency. Give your case a worst-case scenario whereby you wake up one day and – for example – and find your blog is offline. If you had promised your readers a post, they are on your site waiting to read the post and suddenly they can see a thing. Such an issue should be solved in at most 5 to 10 minutes. So if a company took 3 days to respond to your query, then let your readers await at least 6 days for your blog issue to be solved. Now, you don't want that do you? Take keen note on how they interact with you as well, rude or careless customer service is surely not worth your business or time.

Things to Consider When Budgeting for Your Business

Budgeting for a start-up business involves making an educated guess as a projection of what to expect. It's advisable to provide for higher expenses and a low income so that whatever the outcome, you will be prepared. Projections can also be made based on the current geographical area of operation and operating hours based on research.

In an existing business, the previous history of sales and income is used to project average costs in the future. Bank statements and books of accounts are used to come up with budget estimates. You can also make assumptions based on recent market trends for similar businesses.

Determine fixed assets

These are costs that remain constant every month irrespective of an increase or decrease in sales. These are the easiest to determine as you can refer to past bank records. All businesses should have fixed cost agreements that can only be changed by new contractual agreements and not by the performance of the business. Examples of fixed costs include:

- Rent or mortgage
- Salaries
- Internet Services
- Government and bank fees
- Legal services
- Insurance

As much all items must appear on the budget list, you should arrange your fixed cost from the most important and urgent to the least and prioritize accordingly.

Include variable expenses

These are items on the budget without a fixed monthly price tag. These expenses vary in proportion to the production output. Depending on the performance of your business, you will be able to determine whether to maintain, reduce or increase variable expenses. Your monthly profit after subtracting all the costs can be used to increase the variable expenses and thereby growing your business.

Examples of variable expenses include:
- Raw Materials
- Advertising
- Travel and transportation
- Commissions.

- Other marketing costs

The entrepreneur is responsible for preparing the budget both in the start-up and in an existing business. Budgeting tools like accounting software and excel sheets may be used to compare the budget versus actual incomes to measure productivity.

Unique Ways to Come Up with Small Business Capital

With those few tips, you'd be on the right track to a successful startup. Now you have a good idea of how to find great companies to work with and a favorable budget. Do you have that amount at hand?

Disclaimer: Never start a business with only a percentage of the budget. Anything can happen and you may end up not completing your vision. That means the initial amount used will have gone to waste.

So, if you have the whole amount at hand, great! It's time to create your business plan. In case you don't have the full amount or even a free dollar burning your pocket, here are 8 unique ways to come up with a small budget amount.

Savings. This is the best way to fund your business. One, because it is your hard-earned cash so you'll feel the need to put similar effort to the business. Two, because you'll start your business without owing anyone a dime. If you have enough savings use them, if not, give yourself some amount of time to raise the required capital for your venture.

Run a yard sale. Stop with hoarding and use those items to your benefit by holding a yard sale. Depending on how many items you have and how much you'll price them, you may just get the amount you need from a yard sale.

Crowdfunding. Platforms like Kickstarter, EquityNet, SeedUps, and Rockethub are known to be quite effective with getting funds from the public. Once you open an account and express your needs for the funds, why people should help and how much you need in what duration, you may just be lucky and get members to pledge amounts that add to the capital required.

Angel Investors. This is whereby the investor puts money in a start-up business based on your business plan, revenue projections, and trust. Trust can be built through paying back the money on time together with some interest. Accessing angel investors is not easy and therefore you should seek the right contacts and networks. The investor becomes a shareholder and you have a duty to do what is best for the business. However it's important to note that not everyone that invests in the business is the right partner for you.

Credit cards. Credit cards are a fast and convenient way to purchase items required to start a business. It is important to note that they come with huge interest rates for unpaid balances at the end of the month. This means that keeping in mind the business might not generate enough revenue in its early months, it may be difficult to keep up with monthly payments. If you are borrowing for a short period like 18 months or less, it's advisable to pick credit cards with zero or no annual interest.

Microloans. Microloans are credit facilities offered through community-based non-profit organizations. The funds can be used as working capital or to acquire equipment, supplies, and inventory for your business. The loans are repayable within 6 years and interest rates are negotiable between the two parties on a margin of 8 to 13 percent. For you to access the loan from intermediary lenders, collateral or personal guarantee is required. This type of funding is recommended for entrepreneurs who cannot access traditional bank loans due to weak credit scores or limited assets.

Peer to peer loans. Small businesses can make an application for a loan request on a peer to peer lending platform. Investors review and agree on the loan amount after the borrower states the amount required and reasons for borrowing. Previous financial information is used during assessment and therefore a decent credit score is necessary. The loan is repaid through the platform, and in return, the platform pays the investor depending on the agreement made. This form of lending favors small businesses due to low-interest rates and flexible repayment plans.

Friends and family. Your friends and family are more likely to take a higher risk in investing in your business compared to traditional lending facilities like banks. This is because you share an emotional connection with them since they like and care about you. Your family and friends will always be willing to support your ideas and your business.

Chapter 7: Venturing Into Passive Activity with a Bigger Budget

Starting a business does not always have to be a crazy hustle. Sometimes the capital is on the high end and readily available. On the other hand, some passive income ventures may require bigger budgets to start. Don't give up on your passion or ideas just because it comes with a million-dollar bill.

If your passive income idea requires three figures going up in the capital and you have no way of raising that amount, you can always opt to partner up with someone. However, your partner needs to at least be able to raise 50 to 70% of the capital. Why? Because you are the mastermind behind the idea, and assuming you have set up everything required in the startup or investment and all you need is capital only. Be careful with such dealings, though. You can choose to work with a lawyer for the contract agreement.

If you have a large property like a mansion that no one's currently occupying, you can sell it to get capital or take a loan against it. Getting loans is never advisable, mostly big loans, but if you have collateral that you are okay losing, then you can take a loan against it. Even small loans can harm you along the way. If your loan incurs interest and your business idea doesn't work out as planned, your small loan can escalate into a huge loan.

Be wise with purchases. You don't have to purchase all assets in retail. You can purchase some items on a second-hand basis which is always a cheaper option. If you need them in bulk, then get them directly from the manufacturer or a wholesaler. Hire assets that you don't use on a daily basis, and sell off assets that were required on a one-time basis.

Perfect your business plan and budget. Sometimes because capital is readily available, one might end up being extravagant with the budget and unrealistic with the business plan. Use some of that money to hire a business consultant and/or a financial manager to go through your plan and budget and take out unnecessary things that have been included.

When contracting professionals, don't go for those that bill on the high end, unless they can guarantee you success. There are many affordable contractors who perform remarkably well in their services. Survey the industry and make a sane decision. Do not fully pay a contractor for a service not offered. Ensure you have an agreement. Good contractors usually request for money for resources only, then bill you for their service after you're happy with their work. Be keen to read red flags before hiring a contractor.

Start small. Just because you have the money doesn't mean you must start big. Do not get excess stock or higher more than enough employees. The extra money can be used as security money during the grace period. After launching your business, you should give it a grace period of about 6 months to one year. The grace period is the duration to which you monitor a business's performance and see if all is working out or not.

If during the 6 months your business makes nothing but losses, you may have to reconsider the venture. Sometimes the issue comes in with plan loopholes whereby you did not take precaution on certain business matters that are now affecting the business.

Take the first three months to analyze the business performance. If things seem suspicious, spend some of that big budget hiring a business analyst. If after 3 more months the business is still struggling, you may want to either move it to another location or change up the service or product you are selling. All of this will cost you a lot of money. This is why it's important to only spend on necessities when starting. Do not worry, as time goes you can grow your business with that big budget and even open new branches of the company.

Many people become careless with expenditure because they see that there is a lot of money in their accounts. Sadly, investments can run your accounts dry in a very short time if you don't watch out. Big budgets are good and if you want to go big, then spend on professionals to help you and advise you on your journey to investment success.

Chapter 8: 21 Passive Income Business Models for the Year 2020

The following pages will contain 21 of the best passive income business models that will make good money for you. You may choose to take up one or a couple depending on your working team. However, it's advisable to hold on to your day job as you start the idea, planning and startup phase. Once the passive business is stable, then you may go ahead and bid your boss goodbye.

REAL ESTATE INVESTING BUSINESS MODEL

Real estate investing is purchasing land, commercial buildings, and residential buildings with the intention to earn passive income such as rent or profits by selling. In real estate investment, you can either personally search for property, use property brokers, or you can buy the properties online through online real estate market tools.

How real estate investing works

Real estate investing works by capitalizing on the potential in the industry. When you invest in real estate, the potential of earning a passive income is high. Investing in real estate works because the ever-rising population needs shelter and business premises. Therefore the value of properties such as land tends to appreciate due to demand. People are willing to pay you to either rent or buy your property. Additionally, real estate investing can work when you buy a property of less value, upgrade or develop it and sell it at a profit.

When choosing the right property for investment, there are several options to consider which include state of the property, the value of the property, location of the property, and the amount you are willing to invest. Normally, the right property has to earn you as much profit as possible.

Real estate investment has the potential to earn you passive income, especially through rent. When you buy a property and lease it, you earn rent, and you can sell the property at a price higher than the buying price due to appreciation.

How to earn from real estate investing

Real estate investment works in several ways which are appreciation, rent, tax benefits, and interests. For instance, since you can buy a property, hold on it and sell at a higher price. Secondly, you can buy a commercial or residential property and rent it, thus earning a passive income monthly or annually depending on the lease agreement.

Thirdly, as a real estate investor, you can enjoy tax benefits. When you buy as a business owner, you are entitled to tax benefits for repair upgrades or the cost of traveling amongst other benefits. On the other hand, you get interests when you invest in real estate companies or as an investment banker.

Cost Analysis

The cost structure of real estate starts with the market fee of the property which is the price you pay for the property you are buying. In case you would wish to upgrade the property, you will incur an additional fee to the market value. Both the market value and upgrading fees are an on-off payment. The monthly costs you are likely to incur in real estate investing include management and maintenance costs. When you buy a property, especially commercial and residential properties, you are going to incur management costs which will be paid to your property agent. Additionally, you are going to pay for the maintenance of the property. The maintenance fees cater for general repairs of the property.

Real Estate Resources

The main resource that real estate investing is the capital you are willing to invest in. Investing also depends on availability of land because all properties are built on land. Without the availability of land, real estate investing would be pointless. In order to develop property, you can use land that you already own, or you can buy or lease another land. The other resource is knowledge of real estate investing which you can acquire from people around you and online resources such as Roofstock.

Marketing your property

One of the ways you can market your property is through listing and advertising in newspapers and magazines. You are likely to get the attention of potential a buyer or a lessee through adverts in the print media. Additionally, word of mouth marketing works in real estate, either through friends, brokers, and past or existing clients and tenants.

You can also market real estate through online platforms such as websites and social media sites. In order to achieve proper online marketing, especially websites, there is a need to incorporate search engine optimization (SEO) in all online platforms, which will help in ranking highly on Google search

The Real Estate Investing Money-Making Process

The process of real estate investing starts with research on the most appropriate and profitable property. After the research, the next step is buying the property. Buying the property entails paying the market value of the property and acquiring ownership documents from the owner. The next you take is finding potential lessors to the property, and agreeing on the amount of rent to be paid. When acquiring lessees, you have to draft contracts that will stipulate the terms and conditions. The lessees will then pay you to rent either monthly or annually, depending on your contract. On the other hand, you might later decide to sell the property at a profitable price.

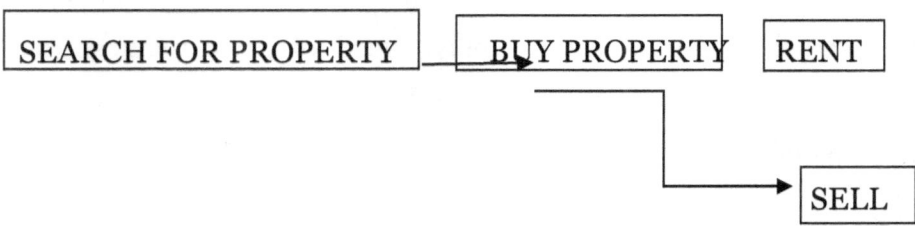

Involved Personnel

There are various parties involved in real estate investing, with each party playing a different role in the process. The parties include property sellers, constructors, managers, brokers, lawyers, investors, tenants, buyers, and construction materials, suppliers. You are the investor, and you will buy the property from a willing seller. You can also construct your property by contracting building material suppliers. On the other hand, when renting your property, you will have to acquire tenants who will be paying rent either directly to you, or through property managers. When selling your property, you will need a willing buyer. Most of the processes in real estate investing require the presence of the layer who will oversee the legality of the processes.

Real estate investing is a worthy venture due to its ability to earn you a passive income. With the appropriate capital and resources, it is possible to live off real estate investing.

Additionally, the rising population makes the venture more profitable since the demand for real estate properties is always rising. Although some people find real estate investing a bit hectic, you can manage to venture into the real estate business alone. However, since the business dwells on knowledge and information, it is more advisable to have partners who are knowledgeable about real estate. Contrary to popular belief that the real estate business if a balloon that is about to burst, the business is here to stay, even past the year 2020.

AMAZON FBA BUSINESS MODEL

Fulfillment by Amazon (FBA) is the advanced seller privilege that allows seller to send products to Amazon's fulfillment centers where Amazon picks them, packs them and ships to customers. This program also comes with customer service, relieving work off the seller. Not every seller is automatically an Amazon FBA member. As a seller you will have to enroll in the FBA program which will cost you depending on the services you'll receive from Amazon's team.

The process of setting up an Amazon seller account

To begin selling on Amazon, one needs a seller account. There are two selling plans; individual and professional. With the individual plan, one is allowed to only sell less than 40 items a month. This would be good for a startup seller to see if selling on

Amazon is the right activity for you. This Individual Plan includes per item selling fees of $0.99 with referral fees and variable closing fees.

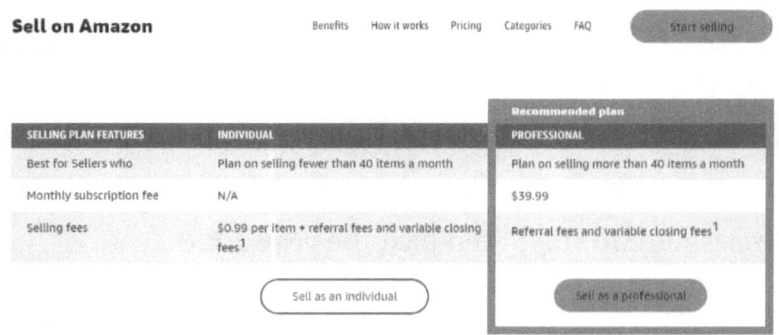

As for the Professional Plan, a seller has the privilege to sell more than 40 items a month. The plan goes for $39.99 renewable monthly fee with no per-item fees. However, it still contains referral fees and the variable closing fee. To get started, all you need is to click on your preferred plan on the Amazon Seller Central page and fill in your email and password details.

The types of products one can sell on Amazon

On Amazon, one can sell anything from electronics like mobile phones and computers to books, furniture, hair and beauty products (those permitted for retail), jewelry and accessories, clothes, shoes and just about any legal product out there. Amazon does not limit the variety of products a seller can work with, hence you get to change up products to your liking. Amazon ships to over 100 countries outside the U.S making a seller's market-wide enough for successful selling.

What makes Amazon FBA a lucrative passive income idea?

Amazon has over one million new sellers every year, yet it makes an average of 100 billion per year. With more than 10 million listed products on the platform, new sellers have a chance to tap into this market and prosper. There are a variety of products so one is not limited to selling only one product. You can market your products from outside Amazon and work from whichever location. You earn as much as you sell; Amazon does not limit the amount of income one can make per month.

How you'll generate money with Amazon FBA

As an Amazon seller, you get to make money from profits in every product you sell. This means that you have to price your products carefully. You cannot price your products too high due to competition and you cannot price them too low because you have to consider profits and business costs. The best way is to get products at a cheap rate. This is successfully done by shipping products directly from the manufacturers in China.

Amazon FBA's Cost Structure

It includes fulfillment fees and monthly storage fees. The fulfillment fee caters to order, packaging, packing, shipping cost. On the other hand, a monthly storage fee is a cost of storing products in their warehouses. Sellers also have the seller fee as separate. Not to forget, Amazon seller account renewal fee of $40 per month.

How to market your Amazon products and rank it with SEO

It starts with the optimization of product listing which involves the title description that should contain; size, material, color, product type, quantity, packaging, name or brand. Important in the optimization is ensuring the use of keywords missing in the title in the product description. Also, it is advisable to create a product description that seems to convey a story.

The product description plays a major role in visibility. In the description ensure to tell your potential clients how your product solves their related problems and use information that'd convince them to make a purchase.

You can also market your products outside Amazon using social media by posting product images and linking to the Amazon product's page. Another method would be to write product reviews on a blog and drive blog traffic to your Amazon products. Other ways include advertising among others.

Amazon FBA's Seller to Buyer Channel

The sales process is quite simple. The first step is to do a product search where you'll select the best products to sell. Once you pick a product, find the manufacturer. You cannot post a product without negotiating costs and partnership agreements with the manufacturer. Once you agree on an amount, you may opt to have a sample sent to you for quality verification. You don't want to sell poor quality products; it'll ruin your reputation as an Amazon seller.

Once verified, price your item. Ensure that the products are at the Amazon warehouse before posting them on the platform. Take HD photos (a manufacturer can also send these on request) and start posting and marketing. From here, a seller spots your product and makes an order including his or her shipping details. The drop-shipping process begins from the Amazon warehouse to the buyer's delivery location.

Earning through Amazon FBA is one of the easiest and most lucrative passive income ideas for the year 2020. It's not as complex, hence you won't need to have a partner to help you run it. You can run this business from the comfort of your home or as you travel since Amazon does not require you to physically handle anything. With capital of less than $100 and promising returns of up to $5,000 a month, Amazon FBA is hands down a passive activity to venture in.

AIRBNB BUSINESS MODEL

Founded in 2008, Airbnb is a platform that allows property owners to provide accommodation for travelers who are looking to enjoy a region's culture by providing living space, Airbnb allows travelers to enjoy a private experience be it touring or a business trip.

How Airbnb works

Airbnb offers a listing opportunity for property owners with spare living space, where hosts monetize these rooms, on the other hand for travelers, Airbnb offers an intimate living solution during your travels. Since its inception, Airbnb has managed to provide hospitality services for about 6 million travelers across the word.

What makes Airbnb unique

- The entire concept of providing travelers with personalized housing is in itself unique but other factors that have made it possible for Airbnb to stand out include:

- Has high profits for the host, the Airbnb host charges the space in nights and not in months or years increasing one's profits, this is unlike real estate owners.
- Unlike real estate business that only offers accommodation, Airbnb is a hospitality business, when we think about hospitality, one thing that crosses our mind is hotels, however, with Airbnb one is able to provide unique hospitality experience.
- Airbnb requires the host to have great sales and marketing skills, this is in comparison to real estate investors, the success of your Airbnb space is dependent on your marketing skills, you need to let people know about your space but as you market your space ensure you stand out with your experience.
- The Airbnb host has higher liability, despite the many advantages of being an Airbnb host there are also several risks associated with this business, to avoid such risk, it is essential for the host to be liable and be on the lookout for any damage on their property.

Different ways to join Airbnb

There are various ways one can join Airbnb as an entrepreneur depending on your location, availability, season and city laws.

You can join Airbnb as *a full-time entrepreneur* and as the name suggest, these kinds of hosts either have a specific space on their property that they make money off, from hosting or other hosts may buy a property dedicated to Airbnb hosting.

One can also join Airbnb as an *opportunist*, these are hosts that may have an extra room in the house and are looking to earn extra cash during a specific time, it may be during a sporting event in the area.

The final way one can join Airbnb as a host is if one *is a side hustle seeker,* the side hustle seekers just like the opportunist take advantage of high seasons. However, the side hustle seekers rent frequently and in some cases accrue a stable income from their spaces.

Pointers for hosting with Airbnb

First, find out how you would like to join Airbnb, for full-time hosts, then you need to be keen on location, find a safe location and serene location. This ensures your clients are safe, comfortable and happy with the experience.

Pricing. Airbnb gives you the freedom to set your nightly prices, however, before setting your price research and find out more about how and when to maximize your prices, also be open to adjusting your prices. Pricing is not only an important factor for the full-time hosts but also plays a big role if you are an opportunist host. Finding out what season increases your returns will have you smiling to the bank.

Insurance, though Airbnb may cover some liability, it is wise to consider additional coverage. As earlier on mention Airbnb spaces are at risk of damage, to avoid high losses consider liability insurance.

Steps to launching your Airbnb business

Airbnb is a great opportunity to earn passive income and will have you enjoying the day to day income with little involvement. So if you are looking to list your space on Airbnb here is a guide on things to consider before launching your Airbnb side gig.

1. *Start by creating an Airbnb account*, the account allows you to customize your space to suit your availability and need

2. Now that you have identified your space the next step is *listing your space on Airbnb then*, set your price Airbnb offers tools that can guide you in deciding the final price by including cleaning fees and discounts.

3. *Choose your availability,* the Airbnb platform allows you to select the time you can host and you can also block dates you cannot host.

4. *Set up house rules,* before reserving a room, let the guests go through the rules. These rules help to safeguard your property and promote harmony during the guests' stay.

5. Once you have listed your space on Airbnb the *final step is advertising.* Proper marketing plays a major role in determining the success of the business.

Rules for hosting with AirBnb

Besides the rules set for the guests, it is important for the hosts to understand the laws associated with renting out space in specific cities. Find out about permits, licenses, taxes and zoning laws in your area.

How to optimize your AirBnb listing

After listing your space on AirBnb it is now time to boost your business, and just like any other business, you need to dedicate the first few months to marketing. Use the first three months as a stepping stone, with proper marketing you are certain to stand out and have good traffic, the AirBnb algorithm favors listings with a lot of traffic and great reviews.

Take great pictures; consider investing in a professional photographer. When it comes to enticing, neat, clear and high-quality pictures play a big part.

Set competitive prices for your space, before settling on a price find out the market price, and set your price accordingly. Also, be open to regulating your prices to suit various seasons.

Get good reviews from your clients, encourage open communication and address any concerns politely and on time, this promotes great reviews, in turn, increasing your traffic and popularity.

FREELANCE BUSINESS MODEL

Freelance work allows you to work remotely and work directly with your clients. Freelancing is wide and one can offer various services from motivation speaking to writing an e-book or articles, creating websites, logos, data entry jobs, tutoring, social media manager to mention a few. The list of freelance jobs is long making it an ideal business venture for many.

Find your area of interest

Starting a freelancing business may be challenging to a new person in the field but after you get the hang of it, you are good too. But first you need to identify your interest, this is the most important step to a successful freelance career. Finding out what you are good at will help you offer gold and in turn get more clients. Remember, freelance workers mostly work on clients so you need to be good and passionate about the services you decide to take up.

Become a master at your craft

The second step to starting a freelancing business is perfecting your art, be a master at what you do. If you are a graphic designer ensure you stand out each time you get a new project and an easy to achieve this is by practicing.

Find a freelancing job

Now that you have identified your art and perfected it, it is time to turn that talent into money. Start the hunting process. In this process, you need to brand yourself, let people know what service you offer and why they should consider you for the job.

Hunting tips; cold pitching, after locating your potential clients do not be afraid to reach out, networking is also another great way to connect with potential clients, also join freelance groups on various social media platforms.

Finding a job as a first time freelance may not be easy but keep on, and use social media to spread the word.

Improving on your craft

After the job search, you will eventually land a job, the final step on how to start a freelance business is ensuring you always learn, improve on your skills. Sign up for lessons and forums.

Top freelancing platforms

There are many freelancing platforms, but before signing in it is vital to understand the company's terms and conditions to decide whether the platform serves your need or not. Some of the top freelancing platforms include;

- Fiverr
- Up work
- Guru
- LinkedIn
- Freelancer.com
- People per hour
- 99designs
- Content mills such as

An alternative freelancing strategy

A good way to start a freelancing business is to use freelancing platforms, though this is not always the case. Joining a freelance platform gives you an opportunity to learn in a safe space, however if you are ready to go all-in, then there are alternative freelancing methods.

One method is creating a website or even a YouTube channel, however, before venturing into any of these alternative methods it is important to be prepared. One way to ensure your freelance business is a success is by branding yourself.

Some people have joined freelance business full time and earn from their websites, to ensure this happens, treat the freelance venture like a business, invest in good logos, have a tagline, including your business email address and you could also add a portfolio of your work.

How to market your freelancing business

There are various ways to market your freelancing business, but one of the most common methods is the use of social media platforms, use social media platforms to spread the word about your services.

Use website portfolios, website portfolios is another great way of marketing yourself, a website portfolio showcases your work to potential clients.

Spread the word, through word of mouth, let your friends, neighbors, colleagues, and family know about your services. A great way to maximize word of mouth is by attending social forums that connect employees and employers.

Rules for being successful with freelancing:

- An easy way to achieve success in your freelance business is by over-delivering, always put your best foot forward and deliver gold, this shows the client that you are devoted to excellence.
- Always deliver on time, this is not only a great way to maximize on your earnings but is also a great way to attract more clients, submitting your work on time or before shows you are committed to your work.
- After offering a service, ask for a review, this is a good way to build trust with potential clients. However, remember to ask for reviews after the client expresses satisfaction in your work.
- Be professional, in most cases, freelance employees and employers do not meet, however in spite of this it is important to be professional and maintain good relations remember to respect different time zones and always be polite.

In the USA approximately 35% of the working population is in freelance business and by 2027 it is estimated that the working population in freelance business will be about 50%. The freelance business has proven to provide financial freedom, do not be left out. You can also become a freelance worker today, all you need to do is identify your craft, sharpen it and present your skills to the world. However, just like other businesses it is important to be patient and committed.

SHOPIFY BUSINESS MODEL

Shopify is an e-commerce software that offers the business a platform to launch and manage their online stores. With Shopify, you can create a website then sell, ship and manage your products. It also has an admin panel, where one can add new products, process orders and manage the store's data.

Why you should consider Shopify

Retail online business has over the decades been made easier with the increased use of the internet, however, despite the many e-commerce stores available it is important to carefully select an online store that suits your needs. Shopify has become one of the leading retail online stores across the globe, this not only gives the buyer's confidence but also allows business owners to reach a wider audience.

In addition to a global audience some other reasons one should consider Shopify as an online shop include:

1. Offers different payments methods

One of the factors to consider when running an online business is the mode of payment; limited methods of payment mean limited sales. To prevent this, Shopify makes sure one can use nearly all payment methods.

2. Shopify has the technical issues under control

Your online store with Shopify is safe and secure, Shopify has it's builtin systems run by professionals to ensure stores are safe at all times. This, however, does not apply to store owners who use WPengine for their WordPress installation. Personal WordPress installation makes the owner responsible for hosting, speed and security of the store.

3. A synchronized platform

Operations are coordinated from, shopping, payment, and inventory. Ensuring the store owner has a good track on the store. This system also enables the seller to keep track of items needed.

4. Offers friendly prices

For a monthly subscription, you pay $29 with no hidden costs this subscription method is however ideal for small and upcoming stores as larger stores pay a higher fee. In addition to the subscription fee Shopify also has a small transaction fee on the small stores; this is however lifted once the store grows.

5. Offers a support team

Shopify has a professional support team, this is unlike other platforms that rely on the community for support. You can always get in touch with the Shopify support team and have issues as well as any inquiries solved.

Getting Started with Shopify

To get started with Shopify, you need to know what e-commerce products you'll be selling. Products can include a specific type such as men's clothes, or a diverse collection like clothing. Other products that can be sold on Shopify include:

- Shoes, bags, and accessories
- Hair products and wigs
- Beauty and skincare products
- Electronics
- Furniture, and more

As the owner of the online store, it's up to you to decide on what products you'll major in. This can range from an activity you love, or a passion you've acquired. With an idea in mind, you can head on to find a reliable supplier.

1. Finding wholesalers/suppliers

Remember your product supplier will affect your entire business model. An unreliable supplier will delay deliveries. An expensive supplier will make pricing impossible for you to make good profits. Therefore, it all comes down to who your supplier is and what policies you agree to work under.

It's advisable to work with local suppliers unless you can locate a reliable international supplier who can ship to you for free or at a reasonable cost. Many choose to get supplies directly from manufacturers or brands. This way it becomes cheaper and easy to compete with market prices while making good profit.

2. Pricing

Now that you have identified your products and wholesale supplier it is now time to price your items. Pricing plays a huge role in determining profit margins, cash flow as well as various expenses the business can afford to cover. However remember, the price you use to launch your business will not be the ultimate price, to set up the price first consider the price you incurred to bring the item to the market, if you are selling your craft, then you need to calculate exactly how much you used to buy the items and time spent on making the item, consider packaging, shipping, commissions, and promotional items, this calculation will give you the total per-product cost.

After establishing the total per-product cost add a profit margin, the profit margin is influenced by the fixed costs, and the market prices, setting higher profit margins might affect the acceptance of your price in the market in turn affecting the sales. The third-factor influencing pricing is the fixed costs, fixed costs are important as they help you break even in the business.

3. Setting up a Shopify shop

To set up a Shopify store, sign up and create an account, after entering the required details click the start button and get a free trial for 14days, you are then required to fill in some more details, your name, country, contact number and address after this step, Shopify will inquire if you have any products you want to sell and your aim. If you just want to try out Shopify to see whether it works for you then you can select, 'I'm just playing around' once done click 'I'm done' to move on to the next step.

On completing the setup process you are directed to the store admin screen, here you are ready to customize your page, setting up payment methods, shipping information and uploading your products. Then choose your layout, Shopify has an official free themes store where users are guaranteed of full support from the designers, you can also access premium fees.

The next step is editing the settings, in this stage, you will edit the themes, add a logo select font sizes, color schemes and number of items to appear on each collection page. For your store to go live, then you will need to pay for a domain name, Shopify charges from $9 to $14 yearly, but one can also buy from a third party.

4. Branding

When creating your brand consider a relatable business name, create a professional logo then get a domain name.

Let people know about your services and products, Shopify makes it easy for the users to reach a larger audience through social media platforms, however, to stand out you need to consistently market your brand, interact and engage potential clients. Additionally you need to have a slogan or tagline, make the tagline catchy, strengthen your brand use testimonials, increases trust between the buyer and seller, in turn, increases one's sales.

5. Policies

Policies are designed to protect the seller and buyer, policies also show your potential customers your commitment towards your business increasing credibility, before creating your policies you need to choose what works for your business.

How to Settle on Store Policies

There are compulsory policies; these are the policies that talk about returns, refunds, taxes, payments, and shipping. You can also include, recommended policies, these policies give warranties guidelines and wholesale inquiries; finally include the bonus policies that touch on coupons, member policies, and discounts. When setting up the policies it is essential to be transparent, and straight to the point this will help avoid misunderstandings.

Upload pictures

Only upload high definition images of your products. Take images from several angles so that a customer can get a good view of that product. When taking the images make sure you have a lighting ring or your room is well lit by sunlight. Also, be sure to use a good camera. To upload your product pictures on Shopify, select 'products', a blue 'add product' button will pop up in the right top corner upload your items and add a small description.

Shopify features that support Facebook and Instagram

Shopify allows clients to easily integrate Facebook and Instagram channels to generate more sales, to connect your Instagram channel with your Shopify store, download the Shopify app, you can download the application on an android or iPhone phone or a desktop

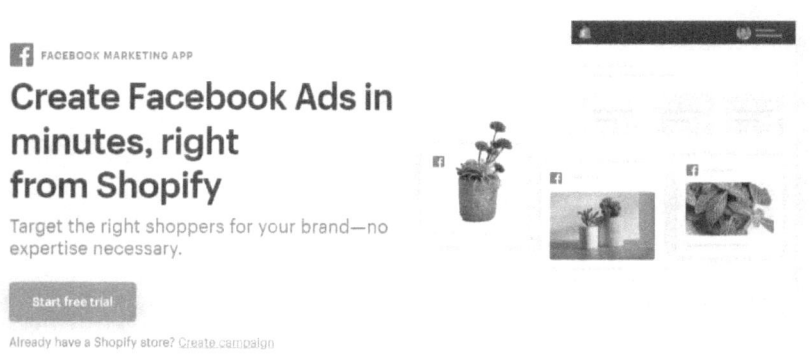

In the application click on the store, tap the plus symbol, then click on the 'add sales channel' and tap on Instagram, log in to your Facebook page to confirm and add the Instagram sales channel.

Marketing your Shopify store

Now that you have set up your online store, uploaded the product pictures, set the prices and policies, it is time to generate sales. Let potential clients know about your products or services on Shopify through marketing. Some of the marketing strategies you can use to increase your audience are social media platforms; creating an email list where you send regular newsletters, email marketing increases repeat clients.

Shopify store launch checklist

Add any sales channels; some sales channels you can add to your Shopify store include eBay, Amazon, social media channels and Google shopping. Sales channels amount to about 70% of all online sales and having various sales channels increases your sales.

- Check the payment settings, you need to ensure customers can complete a purchase.
- Double-check your email notification settings.
- Ensure the images are visible and accurate per the description.
- And finally have a launch marketing plan, before finally launching the store to the world, you need to let people know about your business and expected opening day.

INSTAGRAM BUSINESS MODEL

Instagram is estimated to have more than 700 million monthly users. This makes it the perfect place to advertise your brand since it exposes you to both local and global audiences. You are likely to reach a larger market of your choice without spending a fortune on advertising. You can start your online business to earn passive income since it doesn't have to be something big. Instagram users are known to have a variety of diverse tastes that makes it the perfect place to sell any products that may interest you as long as they are made visually appealing by the camera to your audience. Read on to find out more about conducting your business on Instagram.

How does Instagram business work?

Instagram started as a pictures app and later on incorporated the ability to add videos. Therefore as a seller, all you have to do is post a photo or a video of the product you are selling. Your followers will see the content you post. If they are interested in purchasing your products they will contact you based on the contact information you provided in your profile. In 2016 Instagram can up with business profiles. These are customized accounts to help you conduct business effectively. They provide extra options like promoting your content and being able to attach links for contacting you. Using the business account is more suitable for conducting business on the platform.

Launching your business on Instagram

Firstly, for you to be able to conduct business on Instagram you are going to require an account. This can be easily created following simple steps that are provided once you open the platform. However, after creating the account you will need certain tips for your brand to be successful. Some tips are explained below.

Create a large following before you launch the product. This is all about hyping your product. Influencers can be of help to create anticipation for your followers before the product is officially launched. This is done by giving insights and explaining how the product will change their lives. After all this anticipation you can be sure that your product will sell faster since everyone will be eager to see it for themselves.

Have a beautiful Instagram feed. Instagram is a visual site, therefore, you have to post content that will catch the eye of your target market. Colorful pictures have proved to attract more people than dull colors. Attracting more people to your profile will earn you a larger following and therefore a larger audience for your product.

Interact with influencers. This is proven to be among the first step ways to grow your following. Interacting with accounts that are influential in your industry and have a larger following will help you grow and help you acquire tips on how to conduct business on the platform. It will also attract the right type of audience to your business since you'll be interacting with giants in your industry.

Direct all traffic to your account. In case of any activity that you may participate in that may not be in your account it should all lead to your business account. All advertising and also activity should act as advertising for your business so as to enable maximum traffic to your account and therefore increase followers.

Come up with creative content. The content you post should be simple to understand and eye-catching. The name of your page should be easily memorable and catchy. Come up with interesting and fun hashtags this will encourage your audience to engage in your conversations.

Once the business is ready to come up with offers to keep your audience on the lookout. These are incentives for your audience to always pay attention, they may be rewards or discounts for your loyal fans.

Following the above tips will give you an upper hand in conducting your Instagram business.

What kind of products can one sell on Instagram?

Instagram demand products are mainly electrical appliances e.g. phone chargers and smart home appliances. Organic products and fashionable items are also on high demand among Instagram users.

How Instagram business generates money

The Instagram business generates money when a client buys products from your shop. Instagram shops are mostly just online shops and deliveries done after or before the payments based on your policies. However, some may have warehouses where they store products or store them in their houses.

Instagram business cost structure

Creating an Instagram business account and posting is free. However, in order to promote your products and page, you will need to invest in Instagram advertising. Other costs involved in the business are purchasing the products and delivering them to your customers. Conducting Instagram business is affordable since it's done online.

Resources that Instagram depends on

To be successful in the Instagram business you will require the following resources.

Camera, quality pictures are important to upsell your Instagram. Having a good camera is essential for good photography.

Photo editor, good photographs may not be enough to capture the eyes. Editing your pictures will increase their contrast and brighten them hence making them more captivating to the human eye.

Internet, steady internet will keep you updated with everything happening online. It will enable you to post pictures and interact with your followers efficiently.

How to market your Instagram business account

For your products to reach a larger market you will need to promote them. Products can be advertised in the following ways:

- Promote them so they are seen on the explore tab
- Use carousel ads feature to
- Use Instagram/industry influencers to help promote your product
- Post video ads showing how your products work
- Share pictures and videos on Instagram direct
- Share your content on Instagram stories

Using the above mentioned Instagram features for Instagram your product will reach a larger and more specific audience.

Instagram business partners

Parties involved in the Instagram business are the buyer and the seller. Instagram comes in only to host and advertise your products. Starting on Instagram is free, hence capital needed is only for stalk. This means that you can start and run your Instagram business as a sole proprietorship. Deliveries can also be done individually or you can subcontract someone else to conduct the deliveries. If your products entail a lot, or as your business grows, you can hire a team comprising of a photographer, social media marketer, delivery services, and the like to ease your work.

Instagram business is a very lucrative business opportunity for passive income. This is because it involves very minimal capital. It can also be conducted by one individual at the start but once the business grows it may become very hectic and therefore may need more partners for the business to run effectively.

RENTAL PROPERTY BUSINESS MODEL

Rental property investment is a business model where an investor buys property for the sake of earning from it. You can opt to earn from rental properties by renovating and reselling houses or renting private and commercial spaces to earn rent each month.

How to start investing in Rental Properties

There are several things you need to consider as an investor when you are starting an investment in rental properties. It will be simple for you to successfully invest in rental properties when you follow the key elements. Some of them include the following:

- Be in a rental investment club and seek connections
- Choose a niche and also your rental property market
- Find a way to property secure and finance it
- Do the right investigation and employ a manager
- Establish systems to increase efficiency
- Control the assets and level the enterprise in the right speed

Property survey checklist

Before you start investing in any property it is essential for you to check a few things that will make your investment successful. You should not invest in a property without checking if it will bring you profits or not.

The following is a checklist that you should have before you invest in a property:

- Research the area around that property to survey its security
- Inspect the building's structure to ensure the foundation is at per

- Inspect the building for pests and other insects that might interfere with the comfort
- Find out why the owner is selling the property
- Learn the building's history to know if there's a possibility clients might not want to occupy
- Check for surrounding amenities that might complement living in your property

How renting property generates money

Rental property investment generates money by leasing the property that is divided into units to the tenants. The lease can be monthly or annually where the tenants will pay a rental fee. You should ensure that the rental fee is giving you the required cash flow.

A rental property investment's cost structure entails all the costs you will suffer to maintain and run your investment business well. When you are starting this business you will have to high a team or a company that will act as the landlord. You will be the one paying them because they will be collecting the rental fee form the tenants and maintaining and repairing your property.

Some of the resources that the rental property depends on include the institutionalized banks. There are other ways that they get their resources such as private money lenders and hard money lenders.

How to market your rentals to ensure you always have tenants

When it comes to marketing make sure that you choose the best way that will get you tenants throughout. Some of the ways of getting tenants to include the following:

- Newspapers
- Social media
- Local realtors
- Rental sites
- Billboards
- Previous renters
- Word of mouth
- Direct mail campaigns

There are several people that you will need to work with for you to have a successful rental property business. You need to hire a company or a team that will act as the landlord of your property. Their work will be to find tenants and collect rental fees. The landlord will also be the one doing all the repairs and doing maintenance of your property. In that case you need to hire a manager or a real estate company or manage your rental properties investments.

Rental property investment as a passive income business is profitable if you manage it well and work with the right team. It is not possible for you to work alone because the business involves various things. In that case, you will need a team or a manager who will be helping you with some of the tasks such as collecting the rental fees and also repairing and maintenance. You will also need someone who will help you to do marketing for your properties so that you will have tenants always. When you have good passive income goals you will have a good cash inflow.

VIRTUAL ASSISTANT BUSINESS MODEL

A virtual assistant is online administrative personnel. Just like an office assistant or a secretary, a virtual assistant runs office activities like organizing meetings, customer service and the like. The only difference is that a virtual assistant works remotely because their services are delivered online. This is a good passive income idea where you do the chores you're really good at and earn from them without having to be away from your family.

How to get started with your virtual assistant business

Everything starts with the brand definition. What are you willing or able to offer your clients? You may be diverse in offering several services including social media management, website management, customer service, online marketing, clerical duties, and project management among other services.

While you figure out what you're all about, come up with your business name. Just because you're doing this by yourself doesn't make it less of a business. Either use your name or come up with a catchy but easy to pronounce the name. You can go the extra mile and get yourself a relatable logo and slogan.

If you plan on working with freelancing sites, then the above details could be all you need. However, if you plan on setting your business apart from the rest and getting your own website, then you'll need a domain and hosting.

How to market your virtual assistant services to get clients

Say you've decided to walk away from freelancing sites which provide a platform to grab clients as they come, you will have to spend time and money on marketing to attract clients.

As a sole proprietor, all the work is on you. Fortunately, there's nothing much needed to set up and also, you can always contact professionals to create your logo, website, and social media pages. To market your virtual assistant business, you'll need to go extra on your website and use keywords related to your services in order to rank with search engine optimization.

You can also spend on advertisements on search engines and social media platforms so as to tap into a new and wider community. There's still a freelancing option for when you don't have work. Once you work well with a client, they may just follow you to your website.

Every time you work for a client, request them to rate your work with a testimonial on your website. Also, ask them to refer you to their network. Referrals are the best since the referred clients come to you with information and ready-built trust.

Making money with your virtual assistant business

It all comes down to pricing your services. You can choose to charge per hour, per month or per service offered. Do not set a fixed cost for all your gigs. This is because different clients offer different workloads. Therefore, your pay may end up being too little or too much.

If you offer more than one service, then price each service separately and per hour. This way, every service you perform is paid for and for the duration you've worked. However, always keep your pricing options negotiable. If your gig includes resources like phone bills, ensure it's captured in your invoice to the client.

Go Legal

Register your business and get all the required licenses to start off on the right foot. When dealing with clients, it's important to have them sign a contract before work begins. This prevents collisions later as you work.

Have a business plan and a budget of everything you need to get started with your virtual assistant business. Put your best foot forward and always leave a client impressed by your work, so that they can never hesitate to return for your services.

AFFILIATE MARKETING BUSINESS MODEL

Affiliate marketing can work in different ways. One way is when working with e-commerce sites like Amazon. The other option is to work directly with brands. Because not all brands offer affiliate programs, do not promote a brand's product without consulting them. Deciding to get into affiliate marketing means that you have a blog platform to either review the products on mention them in your posts with a link to their page.

When you become an affiliate of a certain product or brand, then the company pays you as per a certain commission percentage. Some companies may have a fixed rate while others may be open to negotiations. So how does it work? When you talk about a product and link it to its page and a reader redirects and makes a purchase, that's when you get a commission.

Do not confuse affiliate marketing with pay-per-click. With PPC you're paid every time someone clicks on an advert. But, with affiliate marketing, the reader must buy the product. This means that no matter how many clicks you get, as long as they don't convert to purchases, it'll rain stones for you.

Getting Started with Affiliate Marketing

Decide on your business model. Are you an ordinary blogger or a reviewer? Most affiliate marketers choose to review products on their blogs. However, you may still work on your entertainment blog and throw in some links to sell a product. To succeed in affiliate marketing you need solid traffic. This can only be created by constant blogging of interesting topics that attract readers to your blog. This way you have assured at least one person each day will make a purchase.

What is everyone talking about, or what products can bring about a trend? Choose such products as an affiliate. But before you review a product, make sure you see it and at least use it. With that, you're not just reviewing a product for the sake of commissions. To grow readership that is loyal, it's important to show your followers that you go the extra mile to ensure that the products you are recommending are actually worth it.

If you don't already have a blog, then create one, start posting quality content and get active on social media. You can choose a specific industry or review all sorts of items. Once you bring massive sales to a product, get a graphical or representational report of the same. These results will be your portfolio for the next affiliate marketing gig.

Negotiate with Companies

An agreement with companies helps partners to boost profit-sharing as the ideas bring in more selling of the products. You can consult with companies by asking for a raise. Tell the affiliate manager of a pay bump request as through this you can run successful paid campaigns. The increase helps you to have an extra amount of money to work with, thus boosting affiliate sales. The most straightforward route is if you have an affiliate site.

Earn Money with Affiliate Marketing

Coming up with various growth strategies like creating paid Ad sales funnel. Through this, you can scale your business with high profit, as you craft a sale funnel around the products that you are marketing. Creating Ad sales could be done by a boot camp that you give a cheat sheet. The cheat sheet that contains Affiliate links or gives out your email list and you endure that you have a profitable campaign underway.

You can also find more keywords that you can target with your website. You can use a tool like a long trail pro as if your website has more content. It will become more authoritative, and that will make search engines to pick your content more easily. You will earn more money as the search engine will send you more free traffic.

Find affiliate marketing best offers

Start by researching topics for a niche and then narrow down the list. Use a quorum where you can find the trending niche topics. Monetize the issues that are trending on click bank. Use Ad words to research more and find keywords in your new niche that are exploding with growth and high bids. You now start selling your products fast through sites like Amazon and ClickBank.

Success in affiliate marketing

To be successful in affiliate marketing is vital as not everyone has achieved in this business model. You first have to love what you are doing so that you can be able to come up with marketing angles and new ideas. Learn from other partners who have succeeded you can either pay senior affiliates to teach you skills or join affiliate marketing related forums.

You should also learn about the product you are promoting, research the product, and also learn why it is better than its competition. Always have a plan before developing an offer, think about it from a product owner as this will give you the right mindset to look at beforehand.

Build a strong reputation in your niche. Work on building assets and things that have value instead of building a one-page campaign. Stick to one niche and master it. Build your team so that instead of one person, you can have more people bringing in more ideas to the success of the marketing.

Things to do before you start affiliate marketing

Know your audience as you should promote products that match the needs and wants of your audience. Ensure that the products provide a solution to the needs of your audience. You should also be helpful by writing a detailed review of the affiliate product on your site. Use affiliate ads to point them in the right direction if they decide to act on your information. If you have a personal testimonial about the product, include it in your recommendation as it will boost your affiliate sales.

Be patient as affiliate revenue takes time to grow as some programs offer lifetime payouts. You should stay active also in old posts as long as you have referral links as they may still payout. The content marketing strategy should be your prime concern as readers will be interested in invaluable and helpful content. Focus on providing excellent content that will draw customers to your ads and referral links.

NETWORK MARKETING BUSINESS MODEL

Network marketing is a passive income business model that involves sales of products and services from one person to another by independent representatives. Network marketing needs you to create a network of sales to help you sell products and services.

A company or a business that uses network marketing creates a row of salespeople who are required to find their own salespeople for networking. The salesperson that creates his or her own tier of salespeople gets a commission on their sales and sales from their tier of salespeople. The tier can go ahead and create more salespeople but the one on top will be the one to receive more commission as the cycle increases.

How to start a network marketing business

When you are starting a network marketing business the first thing you need to make sure of is that you have enough experience in the network marketing industry. After that determine the level of competition in network marketing and their weakness. After analyzing and doing marketing research you can now venture into the network marketing business.

How to become a network marketer and make money

For you to become a network marketer you need to have an office or a place where you can work comfortably. After that, you will choose the product and services you will be selling. Then start marketing your products and services to the people around you, such as your friends. You can even invite them to join your network business.

You generate money by selling your products and services to your customers. You can also generate money through the people of the dale that you have hired who you will pay through commissions. In that case you will stay at your house while they are doing business for you.

A Network Marketer's Cost Structure

To be a network marketer does not involve a lot of costs or high costs. It is less costly when you work as a freelance network marketer. Some of the costs that you will suffer include making phone calls, fliers, posters, transportation, digital billboards, and internet subscription. You will not have any cost for your office, especially if you are working from home. In that case it is easier for you to start network marketing because it does not require a higher starting capital.

You can use advertise your business through social media, flyers, posters, billboards or even by a word of mouth. Your salespeople can go preaching about your business and you don't have to do it yourself.

You can do the business alone without involving other people. However, it will be more profitable when you invite others to your business. Some of the people that you will need in your business include human resource manager, IT specialist, network marketers or freelance marketers and marketing executive. You will need such a group of people if your marketing business will be large. Salespeople are also some of the people that you will need in your business.

Network marketing can be the best passive income business. It does not involve a lot of work and it is easy to earn from it. If you are starting a big company of network marketing you will need a team to work with to make the business more profitable. However, you can do it alone if you don't want to start a large company. It's a type of business that you can rely on for all your needs because it is more paying.

VENDING MACHINE BUSINESS MODEL

When we talk about passive income requiring less of your time, the vending machine is one of those 'freeing' ventures. Investing in one vending machine may not really bring financial stability to you and your family, but getting a couple of them would be a good source of income. This is the type of business that doesn't require you to have skills or training beforehand. It's quite easy to workaround.

All you need to do is set up the machine and let it work for you. But how can you get started with the vending machine business?

Analyze your business idea

The question is 'what are you planning on selling with your machine?' Hot drinks, cold beverages, milk, water, necessities like tissue rolls, snacks, candy, or bulk vending among other options. Some vending machines can stock a variety; for example snacks, cold beverages and coffee. Starting with your idea in place will help you know the type of machine to get and the best location for your specific service.

Location

Vending machines work best in public settings and areas where there is heavy human traffic like malls, hospitals, near stores, Laundromats, hotels and many more. Whatever location you settle on, ensure it has demand for your product and also surveys the area for security. This is why it's advisable to place vending machines inside buildings with security guards.

Buy a vending machine

Once you get a good location, start hunting for the best vending machine. There are a few places to consider buying the machine; it all comes down to your pocket weight. You can get one from secondary market retailers, which will be a bit costly. You can also buy from resellers as second hand. A second hand vending machine is possibly the cheapest option you can get. However, with this route, you need to conduct a thorough inspection to ensure that the machine is in good condition. Then there's the other option of buying directly from the manufacturer or from wholesalers which comes with a warranty.

Knows the laws & Regulations

What are your state laws for running a vending machine business? Nowadays, you can easily find state laws online, therefore, take time and do some research before setting up shop. There are also ADA Compliance standards that you should take note of before placing your vending machine on public space.

Proprietor agreement

Finally, there are store rules as well to comply with. If the store offers you space, they may provide a proprietor agreement for you to sign. In case they don't then you should. Either get a lawyer to take you through their agreement or have a friend help you brush out word by word. In case you stumble upon a section or even a statement that you do not understand, contact the administration and enquire. Ensure you understand and are 100% with their occupation and payment terms.

Stock your machine

After setting up your machine, fill it to the brim with your preferred products, so as to serve as efficiently as possible. Constantly check on the machine to ensure you fully restock each time. Remember no stock, no income. Also check the machine occasionally to ascertain that it's working as should. In case of any issues, sort them out with urgency.

Before pocketing or banking your profits, also make sure you pay your proprietor to avoid conflict.

CAR RENTAL BUSINESS MODEL

A car rental business entails giving out cars for hire. This passive income business is quite a lucrative model to apply. You can start with a fleet of cars, one car, or even none. This means that no matter your financial situation, your resources are not limited.

Tourist destinations and business hubs are the best when it comes to this venture as people who live there are travelers and require temporary vehicles. However, this business can prosper from any region, as long as you do your marketing right.

The best car for the business

If you do not already own cars, it is important to think about the car service you want to provide and purchase accordingly. The type of service affects the type of car in relation to your target clients. If you are targeting large families, then you have to factor in the size of the car, preferably station wagons with more sitting space and luggage space. Consequently, if your target is businessmen, then a more luxurious executive car should be considered.

Number of cars required

You need to decide how many cars you require depending on your budget and business goals. If you are operating on a small budget, you may begin with one vehicle and expand progressively as the business grows. There is an option of leasing the cars instead of purchase which is actually cheaper. Remember more cars could mean more income for the business if all factors remain constant.

Insurance Services

It is necessary to have insurance services in the car rental business so as to safeguard against unforeseen occurrences. It is advisable to visit an insurance agency to advise you on the best policies for your business. Some of these insurance policies include General liability and personal accident insurance.

Safe storage for the cars

You will require safe and convenient storage space for your cars when they are not in use. If you are starting out with just one car, you can just park it at your home. However in the case of a fleet of cars, renting out a garage space for safekeeping of your cars is very important. It should be in close proximity to your business and easily accessible so as not to keep your clients waiting.

Visibility of your services

To ensure that your target clients are aware of your services, you need to do extensive advertising. You must have a functional website where clients can find information and give feedback. Digital marketing methods like social media should be used to increase the reach. Placing adverts on notice boards close to your target market increases visibility. Such places may include airports, hotels and travel agencies.

Developing a car rental App

You can start a car rental business without a car by developing a car rental App. To get the best from your app you may consider engaging the services of professional developers from Taxi app

Companies. The platform is convenient since it is used by those offering cars for rentals and those looking for cars to rent. The client selects the car they want from your database and liaises directly with the owner on how to get the car. To be safe, it is necessary to install GPS tracking systems so that the location of the car is known at all times

Whether you begin with one or a fleet of cars, the ultimate goal is to provide the best services so as to own a market share as the car rental business is very competitive. Providing for online and mobile forms of payments e.g. Visa and PayPal is a good way to ensure convenience and comfort for your clients. Measures should be put in place to mitigate risks that come with the business e.g. theft.

BICYCLE RENTAL BUSINESS MODEL

Bicycle Rental Business is a lucrative business idea. It does not require a lot of money for a startup, therefore, making it perfect to invest in and earn passive income. It is a seasonal business since it mainly depends on tourists who are in plenty during only a few times in a year. They are mostly located at the beach, in parks or any other areas that are frequented by tourists and college students. Read on to find out more as we analyze the business further.

How a Bicycle Rental Business works

This is similar to any other business all with their upsides and downsides. It is all about catering for people who want to ride bikes from time to time but have no access to them or own them. Individuals hire bikes for different periods of time depending on the errands they want to perform with the bikes. The duration may range anywhere from hours to days or even weeks. It all depends on the policies of your business.

Starting a bicycle Rental Business

Location. The business needs to be located where there is a market and the area is easily accessible. The location should contain a storage area for the bikes or be in close proximity to where the bikes will be stored. Since it is a seasonal business, it is preferable to rent rather than buying the area you intend to conduct the business.

Enough bikes. You do not want to have a shortage of bikes because that is a loss of business. Therefore you need to have enough bikes to satisfy your clientele. If you do not know what to expect, you can start small then grow your fleet with time.

Licenses. You need to have all the required licenses to conduct business in your city. Also have all needed tax documentation and pay all your fees on time. This will make you stay away from trouble with the authorities.

Insurance. You need to find suitable insurance for your business that will cater to insuring all the bicycles you own to protect your business from any accidents that may arise. You also need to set policies for renters of the bicycles to know they are not insured by your business in case of anything.

Promote your business. In order to meet a larger market, you must advertise your business in all ways to reach your target market. This can be done through advertisements in local media, billboard signs, social media and any other places that are frequented by tourists.

Once all of the above are put into consideration you can start your business journey and be ready for the oncoming success.

Target audience

The main target for this business are tourists that may want to tour the city while cycling. College students are also a target market since they are active and may want to use bicycles to visit places within short distances. Any other individuals living in an area that has an active lifestyle can also be your clients.

What resources do I need to start a bike rental business?

For the business to start there needs to be some resources some of the resources are discussed below:

- Bikes and gear. The bikes can either be brand new or second hand depending on your preference. Quality is essential since it determines how long the bicycles will last. Gear such as helmets is important to ensure the safety of your clients and locks to ensure the safety of your bicycles

- Replacement parts. This is because bicycles are bound to spoil from time to time and therefore having accessibility to parts and skills to repair is very important.
- Staff. You will need staff to help you with handling clients. You can also train some staff to also work as repair guys or you could do it yourself to cut costs.
- Rent. This is for the storage space of the bicycles, and gear and also for the display area of the bicycles.
- You will also need professional help to assist you such as lawyers for the agreements and designers for your website and merchandise.

The above resources are just among the ones involved. You can add resources you require as you keep growing in the business.

How to make money from a bicycle rental business

The main source of income for this business is the renting of bikes. More tourists and more bikes mean more money. You can also make more money by merchandising or making deliveries using the bikes that have not been rented at that time.

Bikes Rental Cost Structure

For the business to run effectively different costs have to be incurred. Some payments are only made once, like purchasing of the bicycles. However, most payments are recurring payments, for example, repair of the bikes, rent, salaries for your employees if any and advertising.

How to Market a Bike Rental Business

Marketing is important for every business. For this business, you need to advertise in places that are frequented by tourists. Flyers can be spread at hotels that are frequented by tourists and this will give ideas on where to spend their time. Advertisements can be put on local media to reach students and any interested local. Social media is also a great tool where you can advertise and answer all questions concerning your business to prospective customers.

Business Policies and Precautions to Take

In the case of theft, the insurance company is supposed to compensate your loss. However, proper security policies should be put in place to discourage such incidents. Bikes should always be put on lock when they are not being ridden. Details of the clients renting should also be clearly taken to reduce incidences of theft.

Partnership or Sole proprietorship?

Bike rental business mainly involves the customer and you. You can, however, have partners that provide you with different services like advertising. Bicycles can be obtained from dealer shops around you same applies to replacement parts that you may need. Running the business on your own is only possible when the fleet is small, as the fleet grows you will need help managing heat because the work can easily become overwhelming. Bicycles can be stored in the same area you put the bicycles on display or you can rent a separate secure space where you can store the bikes.

The bicycle rental business is a very lucrative business if done correctly with everything taken into account. It is not always involving and not expensive to begin small. Its ability to start small and keep growing makes it suitable to earn passive income. Follow the above insights and tips to guarantee your success in the bike rental business.

CREATE A PODCAST WITH YOUR SKILLS

As of 2017, a study conducted in the United States of America showed that 40% of Americans and 12 years and above have listened to a podcast and 24% say they have listened to one in the last one month. This makes it a suitable avenue of earning passive income due to the rapidly growing market. However, you may not know how to start your own podcast. Read on to find out all you need to know about podcasts.

How to Start a Podcast

To start a podcast you need to have an idea of what you are going to discuss in the podcast. This gives you the title and enables you to direct your focus to your topic of choice.

Create a brand for your podcast. You can start this by coming up with some simple artwork and a name that. The art should relate to the name of your podcast. This makes it easier to sell and be easily recognized from the art.

After this record your audio, edit it to your liking and it is ready to be posted. Audio files can be hosted on Lisbon, podbean among many other podcast hosting sites. Syndicate your content on an RSS feed to make it available on iTunes and make it available to be streamed and downloaded by your customers

How Podcasting Works

Podcast content can be consumed either by streaming it on the site or blog where it was hosted or on by using a player such as iTunes or SoundCloud since podcast players sync the data from the RSS sites to show the data such as the name artwork and link to the podcast.

Why Start a Podcast

Podcasting targets a market of listeners. This is for people who prefer to consume the written information in audio format. You do not have to be established for you to have a large audience; you can grow with an audience that loves your content as you grow.

You can use your podcast to advertise other activities that you do or advertise for people who can pay you. At the end of the podcasts or in between you can direct your listeners to websites or leave links to the websites you are advertising.

Podcast listeners have been growing rapidly over the years. This makes it a lucrative business to tap into. There are many subcategories that you can venture in to explain your knowledge of the subject. From there people who have been seeking the knowledge will easily find it when they search or the topic.

Once established, it positions you as an authority in your field due to the vast knowledge given. This makes you influential and helps your listeners in purchasing of products you recommend.

Why Podcasting Works as a Content Platform

Podcasts are content platforms since they enable listeners to get information easily while on the go or doing other home activities since it does not require all the concentration that watching videos or reading requires.

Podcasts can listen remotely from smartphones or tablets, this gives flexibility for the audience to listen to what they want when they want. To utilize this you can create a connection with your listeners due to the time they spend listening to you. This will help you push your advertisements more when the audience is most attentive.

Getting Started with your own Podcast

Do your research well and establish the type of content that listeners enjoy and that you are comfortable doing. Check if there is enough information for you to discuss then commit to the theme. Choose the style of your podcasts, it can be going solo or interviewing people choose the one that suits you. Choose the duration of the podcast. Each episode should have around the same duration; this helps your audience to program themselves on when to listen to your podcast.

What you'll Need to Create a pPodcast

Artwork. You will need to come up with attractive artwork for your podcast. Most successful podcasts have very beautiful artwork. You may need to hire a professional for this. The image needs to be large enough preferably 2000×2000.

A name. It should relate to the content being talked about. It should be short and precise. Then thereafter a hook that gives a brief description concerning the podcast.

Category. Choosing the perfect category and subcategory helps your audience find you fast. It also guides you on what to talk about. In case you cannot find a category that suits your podcast, just such for similar podcasts to yours and check the category they use.

Description. Here you should explain everything you think your audience needs to know about your podcasts. This will make it easy to find when they search for it

What Podcast Equipment and Software you Need

For you to start a podcast you are going to need the items below.

Microphone. This is to record your audio. For a start, you can use your phone although the quality will be low compared to using an actual microphone. Better quality audios can be achieved with better quality microphones of anything below $50.

Editing software. This is to edit the raw clip. Raw audio will have lots of unwanted errors or irrelevant information that may need to be edited. There is free software that can help you achieve this to have a clean audio file.

How to Record a Podcast

Plug in the microphone and start talking. In the case of errors just keep talking and the editing will be done once the recording is over. Save it as an MP3 since they have a fixed bitrate, you can also save it at 128kbps to maintain its audio quality while keeping its size small.

How to Create a Podcast: Recording the First Episode

The first episode should be an introduction to the podcast. Talk about yourself a little bit and expectations of the podcast. Be fun. Let it flow naturally, this will give it its authenticity. Having a few points jotted to guide you through will also help to keep you on track.

Have an intro and an outro. This is also a trademark for your podcast. It can be anything from music covers to the episode number. You can make them yourself or hire a professional to do it for you. These help with identity of the podcast.

Growing your podcasts

To grow you need to be consistent in releasing content, this helps the audience to follow through on your content. Advertise your podcast on social media and websites so it reaches a larger audience. Ask for reviews from your listeners so as to know how to improve. Following this will help you grow.

How to Make Money with a Podcast

Podcasts make money through sponsors. These are the clients who pay you for you to advertise their products. Another way to make money is to sell your own products and merchandise by advertising them on your podcast.

Podcasts are free to start and to listen to. If you have a microphone you can record yourself and introduce yourself to the world of podcasting. It may be difficult at first and require a lot of courage but you will get better with time.

SELLING YOUR PHOTOS AND VIDEOS

If you're obsessed with taking photos and videos of nature, animals, streets and buildings, or fine art photography, then it's time to turn this skill and hobby into a lucrative business. With photography and videography, you can choose to focus on one niche or be as diverse as you'd like.

There's nothing more passive than selling photos and videos. The good thing is, if you already have a collection of previously shot images and videos, then you are a step ahead and ready to sell your efforts. There are two main options for turning this skillset into a lucrative venture; selling via your website or selling via graphic websites.

If you'd like, you can extend your job description to custom made photography and videography. This is where a client requests you to take photos or videos as per a certain description or occasion. Either way, you're making good money from your skills.

If you edit your photos, then you have a better chance of selling more and faster. Quality high definition images are always on demand.

How to Get Started Selling your Photos and Videos

The first and obvious step is to do some research and see what others are selling online. Websites like Unsplash have quality photos that can guide you on how to take your photos and make them interesting.

Once you have perused a few websites and *stalked* the best sellers, take a minute and go through your work. Do your photos and videos match the creativity and quality of the best sellers? If they do a good job. In case they don't, try and figure out ways to improve them. This is a good way to also grow as a photographer.

Say your work is great, do more research on websites that pay to submit photos and videos online. Some websites might buy your work then sell to others, while other websites might ask you to sign up and sell your own work on their platform. Once you find a few good platforms, read their terms and policies, learn how they work and read some reviews from members of the platform. If all's well, sign up and submit your work. It's a fact that there are so many websites and so many sellers of photos and videos on the internet. So how can you stand out? The best way is to take your creativity to another level. Like taking photos of birds? Conduct night shoots of birds, capture them in the air, tell a story with your photos and videos by capturing the best moments possible. You can use a theme, whereby all your images have a similar color background.

What about social media? Go the extra mile and provide images that are sizeable to different social platforms. You can also sell images in kits. This is whereby a buyer purchases an image and gets the full social media kit; images of different sizes according to social media platforms.

A Guide to Social Media Pixels for Both Photos and Videos

Instagram. Square images take 1080 by 1080 pixel size. The portrait takes 1080 by 1350 pixels and landscape fits 1080 by 680 pixels in size. Profile picture 180 by 180 pixels.

Facebook. The profile picture is 180 by 180 pixels. Cover image size, 820 by 312 pixels. Cover video image size 820 by 460 pixels for best results. Post image 1200 by 630 pixels with a 3:2 aspect ratio.

Twitter. Profile picture sizes at 400 by 400 pixels. Tweet image size 1024 by 512 pixels with a 5MB size limit. Profile header sizes at 1200 by 500 pixels.

Pinterest. A profile picture should be 240 by 240 pixels and must be below 10MB. Pin image size is 735 by 1102 pixels with a 2:3 aspect ratio.

Using the kit bonuses would boost your work and put you on the front line. However, remember providing all sized images is quite a hustle, therefore ensure you at least cover it in your selling price.

Popular Places to Sell your Photos Online and Aarn

Adobe Stock

As a photographer adobe is a good place to sell your photos since all you require is an Adobe ID. It exposes you to the global market and pays royalties of 33% for photos and 35% for videos. However the payments depend on the quantity sold. Therefore in order to make a decent amount of money one needs to sell a lot of pictures.

Shutter Stock

This is another micro-stock site where users get paid whenever a photo they uploaded gets downloaded by another Shutterstock user. Here photos are relatively cheaper and less exclusive as compared to the other sites. Earnings range from 20% to 30% of the total value of your pictures bought. You can also earn additional revenue by referring to new photographers or customers.

Alamy

This is also a website that gives you a chance to showcase your photography skills. More thoughtful photographs are likely to be bought at a quicker rate. Payments are done monthly only when they are above $50. Photographers earn a commission of 50%, distributers earn 70% while novel use earns 50% of their photos sold.

Etsy

This is a website that allows you to sell printed pictures. You are required to create an account and name your online shop. Then customize it as required and to your liking. Create shipping policies then market the shop in order to reach your desired target market.

Getty Images

This is a high-end sight as compared to other sites. It contains higher quality images that are more exclusive. Earnings are commission-based at a rate of 20%.

123 RF

This is an agency site. It is cheaper as compared to most sites and therefore more difficult to make a lot of money from it. Photos sold in packs ranging from $6.75 to $7.80. Single images range from $0.52 to $0.69. Earnings are commission-based ranging from 30% to 60% based on the exclusivity of the images.

500 px

It is more of a community-based website where you can follow photographers that you are interested in. It makes it easier for your target market to find your work. From there you can earn a commission of 30% to 60% based on how exclusive your images are.

Eye em

This is more of an advertising website. They advertise your photos which makes it a good place for business. You can earn a commission of 50% from selling your work on their website.

Photo Dune

This is a product of the Envato market. Your photos are put on display where they are easily marketable based on your niche. You earn a commission of 30% of the cash deposit of your new referral.

iStock

This is a product of Getty Images. Its standards are generally lower compared to Getty Images. You can also sell your photos on this site. Earnings are commission-based ranging from 25% to 45% based on exclusivity.

Selling your images and videos using your own website

You may opt to go solo and just sell your work via your own website. This becomes a bit advanced and requires more effort and some capital from your end. Good thing is, selling via your website gives you the liberty to price your images or videos as per your liking. You'll get to set your own terms and policies. Clients will be able to understand your personality away from the chaos of thousands of sellers in public platforms.

To get started with a website you'll need the following;
- A domain name
- Hosting
- Website company
- Website theme

You also need a business name and logo for branding.

How to market your photos and videos

To get your work out there, the best way to go about it is showcasing each piece on social media. Open Instagram and Pinterest accounts and start posting regularly. To entertain your followers, you can include a story of how each work came to be. Talk about the inspiration behind it and connect with your followers. Selling photos and videos is a very lucrative business that when done right, can earn you a living.

CRYPTOCURRENCY SPECIALIST

Cryptocurrency is a virtual medium of exchange that is not regulated by any government entity and does not come in any physical form. The most popular Cryptocurrency is Bitcoin. As an example, Bitcoin can be exchanged with tangible currencies like the US dollar because it has value. However, in the United States, the FinTech Law regulates these cryptocurrencies as virtual assets.

A Cryptocurrency consists of a ledger, which facilitates the transactions being made public for visibility. The ledger pushes everyone to be fair and averts the risk of spending double. It basically is a list database entry that cannot be changed anyhow until one satisfies certain conditions.

What a Cryptocurrency specialist does

A Cryptocurrency specialist, also known as a Cryptocurrency expert, is an individual who is well versed in cryptocurrencies and the way they function. This expert individual has the ability to integrate and use the bitcoin network to develop applications.

Who is the target audience?

The target audience is anyone with an interest in blockchain technology and is able to take risks experimenting on it. The future frontier of digital currency is the cryptocurrency and is yet to face more innovation. It also focuses on a community i.e. any group by providing businesses with a reachable market.

How to start a Cryptocurrency business

To get started, one has to first plan the business and register it as a legal entity and ultimately has to register for taxes. Opening a bank account can then follow. This helps in asset protection. To understand business performance, it is necessary to set up accounting systems. Obtaining permits and licenses are also key to enable a business run. Incorporation of insurance policy ensures that a business can still get back on toes in the event of a peril. Taking all the above into consideration, what comes up no is defining your brand and also establishing online presence.

How Cryptocurrency generates money

Cryptocurrencies make money via the initial coin offerings which have the ability to cause a one-time influx of cash in the sale of coins which gain value through popularity and increase in the value.

How to market your Cryptocurrency services

Other than concentrating on technical aspects of coming up with a cryptocurrency, businesses should start by identifying a community likely to use it. This can make them to better get what features most preferred by the community then now incorporate it to the new cryptocurrency and now consider the technical aspects. In some cases, an insurance agency has to also come in.

Cryptocurrency specialist is a business just like the others, therefore, one can depend on it. Despite the possibility of one to run it alone, it could be better if partners are involved as it involves so much making it hectic.

CREATE ONLINE COURSES

For you to be successful at anything, you need to be more knowledgeable about your topic more than the person you intend to teach. You need to ask yourself which topics you want to be known for and those that you have more expertise in.

Choose your course topic

There are definitely several topics you feel most comfortable creating a course on. For you to narrow down to a one-course topic it's advisable to take this exercise. Draw a table with three columns namely skills, passion and interests, and experiences and achievement. Start listing as many things as you can under each column. When you're done, pick at least 3 topics where your skills, passion and interests and experience and achievement meet. For example if you like photography (passion) and you are a great photographer (skill) and you have had a successful photography career (experience) then teaching photography would be the best for you

Identify a specific target audience

Once you have your topic, you need to identify people who have an interest in that topic as your target market. To be able to reach a target market easily, you need to be very specific about what you want to teach. Remember the more specific your course is, the more value it will add to your target audience.

Validate market demand

It would be unfortunate to create a course and then find out later that there is no demand for the same. That is why it is advisable to check the need for your course upfront to avoid wasting time and money on a course that is not relevant. There are 2 ways you can use to validate the demand for your topic.

Research your competition

Find out if there are other people or companies who are selling courses about your topics and who are serving your target market. If there is no one teaching your course online, then there is a problem. It means that there isn't enough market demand and therefore no demand for that specific course.

Ask your target audience what they want to learn

The best way to learn what your target audience is interested in is to ask them directly. Whether you access them online or offline, ask what they would be willing to pay for that particular course. This can be done by asking your social media fans or even subscribers on your mail list. Ask open-ended questions through a survey that can be sent via a link. Consider also reaching them directly via calls or emails and be polite to avoid spamming them. If you cannot find anyone interested in learning your course, you may be required to find another topic.

Create a compelling and unique brand

Once you have identified your course topic, it's time to build an exceptional brand. Take time to design your logo, website and business cards and keep in mind that they represent you and your brand. Make a conscious decision about how you intend to position your brand in the market. It will be easier for people to purchase your brand if you are positioned as an expert in your industry. Think of your brand as the book cover of your business and which the audience will use to gauge your content.

Identify your unique value proposition

Ask yourself who you intend to help, how you'll help them and why it will be beneficial to them. When your audience visits your website, they should immediately be able to figure out who you are, what you do and who your target audience is. You should have a clear and captivating personal brand which will make the reader feel like they are in the right place.

Be strategic with your positioning

Do not try to appeal to everyone, build a brand specifically for your target market. Think of whom you want to attract, how you want your audience to perceive you, and what pushed you to do what you are doing. Your audience should feel like you have helped them achieve their goals or solve a specific problem. To create a good brand, you should identify who you are and what you stand for and understand your target market.

Build your audience

All the people that you are able to reach through a blog, social media or mail list are your audience. It is important to know people who know and trust you since it is difficult to sell without knowing anyone. The earlier you start building your audience the better for your business, it's, however, worth to note that a large audience is good but it is not always necessary. This is because as much as your content will be seen by many people, the most important this is how many engage with you. Loyalty and engagement are the most important factors while trying to build an audience.

How to build an audience online

- **social media**-Have a social media profile on the networks your audiences spend the most time on and engage them
- **Content marketing**-Consider creating free content on your topic to help build trust and authority in your industry and increase exposure
- **Publicity and PR**-Get known by existing audiences by writing popular articles and being featured on traditional media e.g. TV
- **Networking and joint ventures**-Create mutually beneficial relationships with players in your industry

and form partnerships that can lead to greater opportunities.

- **Public speaking-**This can be done by offering to give presentations on conferences and seminars that your target audience attends
- **Email marketing-**Use your mailing list to share your course to people who have expressed interest in your work
- **Paid advertising-**Use platforms like Facebook, Twitter, and YouTube to advertise your business on a modest budget

Creating an online course

Creating an online course can take days or weeks depending on how intense the course will. It might even take months if it contains many modules. However, the process is basically the same as highlighted below;

- Create your course title
- Choose your lesson type
- Create your content
- Edit your content
- Set up your website
- Decide the cost of your course
- Create assignments and discussion boards for your students

- Customize welcome and completion emails for your students
- Create a sales page for your course

Focus on Customer success

Now that you have acquired customers, it's time to deliver to them as promised. As much as you should work towards gaining new customers, you should work to retain the ones you have so that they can come back for another purchase.

DROPSHIPPING BUSINESS MODEL

Dropshipping is a retail fulfillment business concept, whereby retail stores do not store the products it sells. Instead, the products are held in warehouses from where they are transported to the buyer. The merchant does not see or even encounter the goods. They also don't have warehousing costs or even the costs of staffing. There are many success stories on Youtube and Instagram on how to start a dropshipping business. Most of these videos serve as recruitment tools by merchants to get more people to join their dropshipping network and expand their reach.

To start a dropshipping business, the first tool to use is an integrated product marketplace and an E-commerce platform. Though it is the merchant's choice on which e-commerce platform to use, it is advisable to use platforms that have a lot of traffic because some of these platforms will offer free advertising to goods and services that are in high demand. Starting a dropshipping business is similar to starting any other sales enterprise. The critical components required are A marketable concept, sales channels, a source for goods and a marketing plan and tactics. The main advantage of the dropshipping business over other sales enterprise is the very low costs it takes to set it up. Inventory, Staff and storage facilities dot feature in the dropshipping business.

The dropshipping business sounds like the perfect business plan for people interested in making quick, easy cash that requires low capital. However, like many other businesses, dropshipping requires discipline and tactics to compete against other bigger players in the market. The following five tactics come in handy when starting a low-cost dropshipping business:

1. Develop a marketable business concept

Any successful business requires marketable business concepts. The products and services sold via drop shipping are available to any third party willing to market the product and create a sales channel that attracts many buyers. A marketable concept may be in the form of nifty advertising or by-product association with another popular product. For example, selling energy drinks alongside gym equipment is a marketable business concept that works in favor of both product sales.

2. Explore Dropshipping Suppliers

With a great concept in place, it is now time to identify the right suppliers. For starters, engaging direct suppliers can be difficult and increase marketing costs. The best and cheapest option is to identify a good marketplace and signup. Most marketplaces provide a platform where suppliers and merchants engage in predetermined rates and agreements. Most drop ship marketplaces such as AliExpress, Oberlo, Printful, and Modalyst offer free signups for starters.

3. Build Your Dropshipping Website

For your dropshipping business to really take off, the next step is to develop your own E-commerce website. On this website, a merchant showcases the products and services they feel comfortable marketing and selling. Choosing the right website design and functionalities depend on the overall business concept and the supplier plan. Some e platforms are optimized for product-based business concept whereas others are optimized for concept-based concepts. It is important to weigh the pros and cons of various e-commerce platforms based on what people are saying online and also by practically using it to source for goods.

4. Add Drop Ship Products to your site

Choosing the right product to offer can be the difference between a successful dropshipping business or a failure. Factors to consider before populating your website with products are:

- Item Popularity
- Shipping Costs
- Supplier Reliability
- Profitability
- Item Quality
- Return Policy
- Supplier Reliability

Some of these factors may be more important than others depending on the nature of your business model and your preferred market.

5. Market and Manage Your business

Marketing is the only aspect of a dropshipping business that requires some money. In fact marketing in any business should have a directly proportional cost to expected revenue. Paid ads and Social media marketing have the best return on marketing investment for the business.

The goal here is to use simple marketing tools but to also optimize their efficiency by paying for advertising features to target markets that would be difficult to directly appeal to. Managing a drop shipping business requires vigilance and attention to detail. Ensure customers receive their goods in time and in the condition they ordered.

In conclusion, dropshipping is one of the fastest-growing industries that uses already established supply chains and tools to build individual supply business.

CREATE A BLOG

Blogging is when one writes about regular events and situations on their online platform with the intention to educate, inform or entertain the public. The online platform is known as a blog. It resembles a website; however, the whole interface is dynamic and designed for daily content updates. A person who blogs is referred to as a blogger. Readers following a blog and its activities are referred to as *traffic*.

How blogging works

Depending on your business model, you may decide to publish posts on your blog every day or a couple of times a week. It is always advisable to post at least once a day to keep your readership on the upper side. Constant posting also helps in ranking the blog on search engines. The most important thing you can do with your blog provides quality and factual information to avoid misleading your readers.

Blogging entails writing content, recording audios or taking videos and photos that accompany that blog post and publishing on the website (blog). Just like the written post, audios, videos and images must be of quality as well. Sometimes as a blogger, you may choose to use stock images, infographics, and other varieties of graphics to color their posts and make their message better understood.

The process of starting a blog

Starting a blog is more or less similar to starting a business. In fact, to earn with your blog, you must consider it a business and manage it like one. That said, here is the starter pack:

- Blog name
- Business logo
- Slogan (not mandatory)
- A domain name
- Hosting
- A blog platform (WordPress, Wix, etc)
- A blog theme (some are free, others premium)
- A blog developer (in case you don't know how to optimize a theme)

Depending on the hosting provider you choose, you may be lucky enough to find most of the above services provided under one roof. In case your preferred hosting provider only sells domain names and hosting, then feel free to outsource the other services. You can browse for companies that offer such services. You may opt to start with free blogging platforms like Blogger, Medium, Wordpress.org and the like. Promoting free blogs is not quite easy or professional, so you may want to stick to appearing like a real business.

Topics to blog about

There are a lot of bloggers and you are free to choose the blogger you want to be. Some bloggers blog on general industry topics; for example in the health industry such a blogger would incorporate posts on healthy meal recipes, supplements, working out, weight loss options, etc. Another blogger would choose to narrow down to a specific topic (also called niche) and only blog about working out.

To choose the best topic that would end up being lucrative, it's advisable to go for something you have knowledge or skills on, or a topic you are truly passionate about. This way, you already know what you are doing and being your passion, you can drive through industry challenges.

What makes blogging a lucrative passive income idea?

Blogging can be very lucrative, mostly if you settle on a niche. You will find tons of opportunities to make money with not only your blog but also yourself as a personal brand. You can go ahead and come up with products and services from that specific niche as well that will bring you money. As a blogger, you'll never run out of ways to earn.

How blogging generates money

As mentioned, there are various ways to make money with your blog. Take note that a blog and its accessories (like social media) can make up to 3 figures in less than a year. However, this will depend on how you present your brand to the world, and how you market yourself.

The first probable way of making money with a blog is through Google AdSense. In a month after launching and posting severally, you can register for Google AdSense. This is where Google places relevant advertisements on your blog and pays you for every click on the ad (Pay per Click)

With a great blog and social media popularity, you'll be able to land yourself corporate gigs of product placement and ambassadorship. This is one of the ways to make over $10,000 in just a month. However, you have to go the extra mile and present yourself to high paying brands.

If you have a YouTube channel, you'll be able to make money through YouTube advertisements. Companies can also approach you and sponsor your YouTube videos for a product mention.

You can also come up with eBooks, training materials and start selling products related to your niche. For example, if you blog about exercising for weight loss, you can launch supplements that help in the weight loss process and sell to readers. If you run

AdSense, do product placements, affiliate market, sell products, become a brand ambassador, and all those activities, you may just be able to earn 3 figures in a month.

A Blog's Cost Structure

It all depends on all the activities you're running using your blog. However, if you're only blogging with selling materials and whatnot, then your monthly costs would include:

- Hosting renewal
- Blog advertising (on Google and Social Media)
- Content creation (if you travel and if you have a content team)
- Photo editing software (if you use those that renew monthly)

Initial budget with one-off purchases would include things like buying the blog theme, a camera for photography, a good phone for social media and taking photos as well, and much more. All these will depend on your niche and what the industry expects from you.

How to market your blog

Not every blogger makes money with their blog. This is due to the lack of the essential factor – traffic. To attract more readers to your blog, you can do some marketing. The easiest type of marketing is content marketing which involves use of content materials like graphics and text to create popularity of your work.

You can go for good old advertising and spend some money promoting your blog using Google AdWords, social media promotion features and more avenues. You can also use social media to create popularity to your personal brand which in turn sends traffic to your blog.

Developing your blogging team

A blog can be run solely by one party. However, as you grow and get busy with promotions and creation of products, materials or services, you may need to hire a team.

- Content Editor
- Photographer (who should also be a photo editor)
- Videographer (if you'll feature videos; they should also know how to edit)
- Social Media Manager
- Personal assistant (or a manager to get you promotions and organize your activities)

Blogging is hands down one of the best passive income business ventures that you not only have fun making up but also one that can make you good money in a short period. You don't need massive capital to start off, no education required except knowledge and skill, and you can do it all by yourself without the need to partner with someone. It's also a full-time business that can adequately finance your life.

Conclusion

Thank you for making it through to the end of *Passive Income Ideas*, let's hope it was informative and able to provide you with all of the tools you need to achieve your goals whatever they may be.

The next step is to start envisioning a better future for you and your family while you get ready to venture into the passive income business of your choice. Consider your favorite activity, your passion, knowledge, and skills as you pick the idea that'll bring you the financial freedom you've been yearning for. Don't hesitate to do some research to see what others in that industry say about the business.

Remember to always stay open-minded and ready for any surprises. No matter what business venture you take up, you'll always meet a few challenges. Don't let them weigh you down, maintain a positive mindset and everything will eventually work in your favor.

Use the SMART formula to achieve your goals and targets and don't fear to go big with your budget. Investing is very addictive. Once your first investment brings you massive income with just little effort on your end, you'll be willing to invest more, even in different industries. Don't shy off, power on and change your life for good. Be willing to take risks and learn as you go, and with no time, you'll be out of your day job and giving motivational speeches on investing.

Finally, if you found this book useful in any way, a review on Amazon is always appreciated!

www.ingramcontent.com/pod-product-compliance
Lightning Source LLC
Chambersburg PA
CBHW021415210526
45463CB00001B/383